T0304566

SETTE:

SEVEN WAYS THAT THE "ECONOMIC ROYALISTS"[1] HAVE "SEIZED OUR COUNTRY"[2]

DOMINIC M. MARTIN

iUniverse, Inc.

New York   Bloomington

1   Franklin Delano Roosevelt on June 27, 1936 accepting his party's renomination.
2   Economics Professor Simon Johnson of Massachusetts Institute of Technology, quote taken from his article in Atlantic entitled "The Quiet Camp" May 2009

Sette

iUniverse books may be ordered through booksellers or by contacting:

iUniverse
1663 Liberty Drive
Bloomington, IN 47403
www.iuniverse.com
1-800-Authors (1-800-288-4677)

ISBN: 978-1-4502-6187-6
ISBN: 978-1-4502-6188-3

Printed in the United States of America

iUniverse rev. date: 10/22/10

Table of Contents

Author's Note

<u>Sette</u> (7) is meant as a companion piece to my earlier book, <u>Undici</u> (11). Yes, I wrote them in backward, non-chronological order, but, what the dingus! Both numbers, 7 and 11, are roundly evocative and always conjure luck. I imagine both books printed together, published handsomely, produced with only the finest stiff buckram and azure blue calfskin, sold as one unit, united by a red, white and green (re: Italy's tricolor flag) slipcover. I also imagine flying pigs and bees that march in unison. One might as well go down blazing.

The astute reader may note that both works are soldiering ones, teams marking battleground sorties, or wars with words. To soften the diatribe some humor is attempted since "Small cheer and great welcome makes a merry feast."[3] I cannot go five steps without Will. Mirth, again, becomes a feast, and that's just tickety - boo with me. You? Let us march onward, into the fray.

---

3   <u>The</u> <u>Comedy</u> <u>of</u> <u>Errors</u>. William Shakespeare. III.1.26

Avarice, envy, pride
Three fatal sparks

Dante Alighieri
<u>Inferno</u> Canto V, Line 74

Whatever you have, spend less.

Samuel Johnson
Letter to Boswell.
December 7, 1782

The only lobbyist the whole people have in Washington is the President.

Harry S. Truman
Quoted by William Safire.
<u>Safire's</u> <u>New</u> <u>Political</u> <u>Dictionary</u>. P.93

A Jump to a Junk Conclusion

George Armstrong Custer (1839-1876) made many false assumptions, at least, three. He assumed that fellow officers Reno and Benteen would return in time for the battle. He assumed that the Sioux would not be willing to fight with alacrity or vigor. And, finally, he assumed that the Sioux did not posses the Winchester, lever-action, repeating rifle. Early in the battle, therefore, he must have asked himself how the Indians had gotten this new and advantageous weapon, and, yet the 7th Calvary, which he led, did not. Later, as he was about to die and, then be scalped, he must have wondered: "Who sold to them these damn guns?"

Preface

When, close to 30 years ago, I needed to buy a pickup truck for work, my father asked me how I was going to pay for it, or, "get the needful" as he called it. I told him that I already had half the needed amount saved up ($2500 - Yes, all was much cheaper then!), but that I needed another $2500 to seal the deal. He posed the question, "How are you going to get it?" I responded, dully, "Go to a bank, I guess." He instantly frowned, furrowing his tanned brow, and said, ominously, "Don't do that. They are a bunch of crass bastards. Let's talk. I think we can help you out a little. Don't go to a blooming bank." And so, it turned out that my parents, long ago now, kindly loaned me the money and I bought the small truck, soon to be beaten and broken, thrashed about and abused; and during that necessary and common mistreatment, I paid a miserly sum back to them monthly. Finally, at the end, once the principle had been completely returned to them, I asked my secretary at work to make a rough calculation of how much interest had accrued, and, in my last note to them, I paid back to them that amount as well.

Yet, the larger question arises: Why did my father, <u>a banker</u> <u>himself</u>, so strongly urge me to eschew them? Is it because, as John Kennedy said, "All businessmen are bastards."? Or, in giving to me that sage and surprising advice, was my father, someone who would have been just 15 years old when the Depression first hit, recalling the thousands of foreclosures on homes and farms, indeed, on all manner of business back in his hometown of Duluth, Minnesota that he had seen? As a teenager, had he not witnessed them, and later recalled again, the resulting deprivations, the pressured squalor and mean anxiety of poverty?

More than anything, and like many of <u>The</u> <u>Greatest</u> <u>Generation</u> (re: Tom Brokaw) he did not <u>trust</u> financial institutions since he had seen with his own eyes, as an impressionable teenager, what so many of them had done to regular people, how millions of average lives were altered, fundamentally, overnight. When we spoke of these issues down through the years (and we did often and loquaciously, so great and close, eventually, was our brotherly friendship), he always to me said, "Cash is king! Don't be a high roller. And don't buy something, hot shot, unless you can pay for it up-front. The needful. Except your house. Do you hear me, thunderbird? Or, will you forget that, as well? Ding how?" Today, his words still echo in my head and roll around my brain, informing even these disparate comments, marking a spectre of bleak foreboding all encircling and once neglected, lessons so simple to which, earlier, I might have paid a much more focused attention.

Speaking of attention, if my father were alive today, what factors would hold his focus and concentration, steal his resolve, infuriate his mood, set fire to his Irish temper? If he would learn that 40% of Ivy League graduates immediately (that is, up to the recent meltdown!) receive very high paying positions on Wall Street, what would he say? Would he declaim and rail against that high percentage? Would he look at the 2-tier wage system in the country - the fact that financial institutions generally pay salaries and bonuses stratospherically above most other employment - and urge wage curbs? On what basis? Would he look towards the boards of directors for some constraining impulse? What would he or, indeed, any of us say to the argument made by the government (and others) that failing banks are "too big to fail[4]?" As someone who went through the Depression and World War II, he would, I now know, scoff at that poor excuse. Having not had any easy life, he did not care much for excuses, or, what he called from his navy years, SNAFUs: Situation Normal All Fouled Up.

Frankly, he would go beyond scoffing. He would say, if he were alive today, that the banks' reasoning - that they must be saved else all others will equally perish - is bogus and self-serving. He would say that if anti-trust laws had been properly enforced, banks would not have become so Gargantuan. He would further say that the moneyed would have handled these collapses in their own way, and that taxpayer monies should never have been used to bail out poorly run, overly aggressive ventures. He would say: The cookie should have been left to crumble, and the mice would have gathered to nibble at the bits leftover.

All ask: How did this happen, that the banks now tell the government what to do, instead of the other way around? That question is the central one to which this book is addressed. In studying that question and explaining its answer or answers for rightness, lessons will be learned that are crucial for our nature's turnaround, survival and,

---

4   The phrase is taken from Gary H. Stern and Rob J. Feldman's book <u>Too</u> <u>Big</u> <u>To</u> <u>Fail</u>: <u>The</u> <u>Hazards</u> <u>of</u> <u>Bank</u> <u>Bailouts</u> Washington, DC: Brookings Institution Press, 2004.

need one even now say the word, prosperity. If those lessons are not learned and acted upon, I, as well as my father from the grave, fear the worst, that we shall never recover economically, that the 2-tier wage system will only continue, and that a lazy government will continue to be subordinate, all conditions which do not bode will for that "forgotten American" as FDR called him, the common man.

If asked, I suspect, my father, the banker, may have admitted to some small, incipient embarrassment at that employ: It was not manly enough, and it made no real product. Banks create only speculative, not real, wealth; and speculative profits, as we have seen in 1929 and 2008, may disappear like smoke up a chimney in a matter of days. Sometimes, too, he told me of banks that made disproportionate, inordinate profits and he did not like that, believing that they should do more for the community in which they were based.

So, to tame that middling shame, as a banker he was always very careful about the fortunes, the prospects, and the future of his customer. He certainly protected the customer more than most other bankers did. He actually <u>cared</u> <u>about</u> their financial fortunes and future. He never let a loan for its attendant fees, and scolded those around him who may have tried to do so, "Don't milk the system!," he would decry. "Not at this bank, you churner!" he would bellow. He would never loan money to families who were on the fence financially. He would always ere on the side of caution, advising clients to "come back when the sky is a little bit more clear. Then, we will help you out. I promise." He understood that all business is a 2-way street, and that banks must help people and not merely generate loan fees. He understood that in all financial relationships a "window of fairness" must exist and that any deal outside that window fundamentally harms that relationship; and, further, that if that relationship between the bank and any given client is damaged badly enough, eventually the bank will have nobody to bank to.

Thus, it is a good thing that he is no longer with us. He would be more than aghast at the over-lending, the trolling for fees, the ramshackle, sloppy ways that the smallest details are often mishandled. He would not be able to hide his embarrassment at his trade and would, therefore, no doubt choose another. In short, he actually cared and worked for the customer <u>as</u> <u>well</u> <u>as</u> the bank, and if it were no longer possible to avoid these new and dangerous exigencies: Place that dangerous home equity loan, secure that jumbo home mortgage with the 3rd year jump-up in rates, fudge the income and collateral, and all the other little merry tricks which have become so common, then he would have demurred and fallen away, saying: "No. I must now try my hand at something else." His morals or standards or intrinsic fundamentals would not have allowed him to participate in today's gaga banking world; but, in any case, <u>if</u> he had briefly tried to do so, the higher-ups would have labeled him a dinosaur, someone hopeless and confused and recalcitrant, a throwback, a slowpoke, or anti-mountebank or financial Luddite, someone who was not with it, or cold meat. He might have been pleased at all those charges and, even today, I may see the slight Irish smile growing, on his tanned, wrinkle-less face.

* * *

Ten years ago, our family business of 40 years having been sold, the Bank (which for the purposes of this humble work need not be named, so intent is this work's purpose to educate we natives and not merely decry one particular institution) approached us. The Bank wanted to invest our monies carefully and prudently, or, at least, so they said. We would have only one manager who would attend to our account, guarding it judiciously, as if it were his own. The Bank would neither gamble nor be tricked. It would astutely anticipate all market moves and assiduously protect all assets from any and all precipitous losses. Profits would be large and the rate of returns would be at least 2% greater than that for bonds. It was based on these pledge or warrants or promises or guarantees that we, like a young and hungry fish, took to the hook.

So heightened was their aggression, so florid their gregariousness, that they, these bankers forecasting the future and all that they would do for us, began to appear nearly as panderers or sycophants. To curry favor or to ingratiate - all to land the fish - where would they stop? At one point I asked whether they could anticipate, and thus avoid, all steep market declines. The experts' eyes narrowed and one said simply, "That is our job. That is why and how we are the experts." The word "Hubris" then came to my mind, but I was not quite sure of its meaning. I thought, "Is it a cousin to arrogance, or a brother to pride?" I resolved to look up the word in the dictionary and to never again forget its meaning, to fold it into my brain's deepest recesses from which, any time later, I might retrieve it and put it to some proper, steeping use. Later, I found it and thus here record. Hubris: Overbearing pride or presumption; arrogance; from the same word in Greek meaning insolence or outrage.

Yet, what stranger, filled with a fomenting pride, thinks it so? Does pride necessarily not blind, with neither coarse nor scarce warning? Who is to judge an actor or an action; does that not come later and not by me?

To again demur: Some must. Am I to judge? William Shakespeare writes in <u>Othello</u>:

"O heavens! That such companions thou 'dst unfold,
And put in every honest hand a whip
To lash the rascals naked through the world."
Act IV; Scene 2; Line 148

A flash of thunder ranges across the nightly sky. Is it heard? By whom? No malarkey. I turn often to William Shakespeare because he is smarter than I zounds.

Turning a bit further, as will be seen, I shall use Shakespeare's words throughout this ripe trifling since, simply, that use is most apt. Clearly, he thought lengthily and deeply about treachery and money, honesty, false promise, posturing, fudging, conniving, prevarication and mendacity's uneven edge. He must have felt, especially early on when his reputation was only tender growing, the strict pressures of money, of rarely having enough of it, and, too, how easily it can melt away, like trying to hold a quantity of water in one's shallow cupped hands. Throughout his texts, sprinkled nearly everywhere but especially in the histories and tragedies, there are near endless samplings of these words which all relate to money, how it may be nefariously accumulated, how it may slip away, or how it can be used for the common good, if so uncommonly. Examples:

How absolute the knave is!

Hamlet V.I.137

Be checked for silence

But never tax'd for speech.
All's Well that Ends Well I.I.67

And greedily devour the treacherous bait.
Much Ado About Nothing III. 1.28

Custom hath made it in him a property of easiness.

Hamlet V.I.67

My man's as true as steel.

Romeo and Juliet II.4.194

Well, honor is the subject of my story.

Julius Caesar I.2.92

The wealthy curled darlings of our nation.

Othello I.2.69

Away you scullion! You rampallion! You fustilarian!

I'll tickle your catastrophe.
Henry IV, Part 2. II.1.58

Constantly in his work the themes of honesty and betrayal converge, meld, weave, so much so that I wonder if in his own life he did not suffer converse relations with past friends over money, debts uncollected, sums deviated. His insights are central to this small narrative since they show that he pondered the same questions as we do, but 400 years ago.

William Shakespeare obviously thought deeply about how one ought to lead one's life, what constitutes fairness and stupidity (Knavery and skullduggery!) and what sort of blows a friendship might endure before it is forever fractured. He writes constantly about what bonds, fragile and invincible, hold us together, and what sort of personal behavior is required if one may earn that meager moniker: Decent. Obviously, he continually writes about treachery and betrayal, shysters (Re: Shylock from The Merchant of Venice), the growth at mendacity's hip, and the unseen, yet corrosive, effects of greed and larceny. True to say, he praises guile, yet only up to some obscure, undeclared point of mischievousness since, beyond it, a man ventures into dishonesty. So, he tempts us, always: Where is that line? Finally, he discusses how the more fortunate must help the less so, to earn that station's wealth anew. For all of these reasons, I have included many short lines from his plays.

This short work is not meant to castigate or defame any one bank. Rather, it is meant to provide a needed understanding of how this economic meltdown of 2008 occurred, or else, it will surely take place again. And, unless we grasp, as Simon Johnson says "How bankers seized America", we will not know how to wrest her free. And, finally, if we are no longer free, what good are we to ourselves or any other people around the world?

The reader may correctly ask: How am I qualified to speak on these issues? My father, educated in economics at the University of Minnesota, talked about money at the dinner table nearly every night. He discussed the French franc and compared it to the Swiss franc all the time. In 1956, when the Common Market was first formed, he knew intrinsically that that new entity would go toe-to-toe with the United States, that, then, Europe resented our dominant power in the world, and that one day the Common Market (later to be the European Union) would adopt a common currency which he believed, for once mistakenly, would be the German Mark. He understood that the Common Market would lead to government doing more and more for people, that it would creep more and more towards socialism, and as someone who believed in capitalism, while understanding that it must be guarded and controlled by alert government regulation, this tendency made him both sad and angry, down or jump salty, to use the unique Navy argot that he picked up during the war. Especially, he grasped that corporations should never become more powerful than the country. And, finally, he comprehended that all salaries must be earned: An honest day's wage for an honest day's work, and someone should not get paid much money for "skimming" or "churning", i.e., activities which do not promote the general good. Even then, while I was still barely above his knees, he pronounced that, "These jerks make way too much money for doing too little real good, hear me, little shaver? A bunch of hooey!" Soon, I knew that he was pretty damn serious, because he kept repeating himself all the time, saying words like: "Out of line," "screwed-up," "slime," "money-bags!" "freeloaders," "grifters loaded for bear," "leeches," "horsefeathers!" and "lazy lords!" And soon, too, like most sons, I suppose, I had taken on near all of these attitudes and prickly pronouncements as my own. Finally, here, I can perhaps give back to him some of the credit for all that he did for me: The gifts of thought and questions, the careful fatherly advice and the wonder of his language, colorful and profane and special only to him, that, otherwise, I never would have heard. If successful, this hatchway story is an investigation not just about how one bank lost its way (poor thinking, hubris, avarice, etc...) but about how our financial institutions have become a part of one fused oligarchy, and about how they, now it, manipulate corruptly the government to achieve ever greater focus and control with every passing day.

Not a harangue, I aim the tale to be conversational and entertaining especially given the subject which is, admittedly, as dry as Melba. It ought to have the friendly, garrulous tone of a guy in a bar who thinks, "I have yet room for six scotches more", but who has only taken one! (William Shakespeare. <u>Anthony</u> <u>and</u> <u>Cleopatra</u>. Act IV. Sec 7. Line 9) Too, battalion leaders, admirals, and doges of the palace know that, first, one must recognize the enemy before any battle plan may be developed. So they ask us: Are we ready for a war? After we have studied this corruption, can we still use our brains? And, can we fully commit to battle? They might say: If something is rotten, it is rotten to the core. Or, using the old Italian saying: The fish first rots from the head. And that if one's heart and mind are free, one must have the courage to use them to the end of all arguments. So thought William Wallace in protesting the English tyranny upon the Scots 700 years ago. He knew, as we must rediscover, that without freedom we are all lost. So, then, here we go, into the muck or mire.

> Radix malorum est cupiditas
>> Greed is the root of all evils.
>> I Timothy vi 10 in the <u>Vulgate</u>
>> Quoted in Chaucer, Prologue to the
>> <u>Pardoner's Tale</u> VI (C) 426

> If one can no longer trust the government to do the right thing, to whom does one turn?
>> DMM

> All the contact I have had with politics has left me feeling as though I had been drinking out of spittoons.
>> Ernest Hemingway
>> <u>New York Times</u>. Sept. 17, 1950

Chapter One:
Collusion at the Oligarchy

Please recall those two words which are at the center of our debate:

> Collusion: A secret agreement or understanding for purposes of trickery or fraud; underhand scheming or working with another; deceit, fraud, trickery; where the prince and the police stand together in foul union.

> Oligarchy: Government by a few; a form of government in which the power is confined to a few persons or families. Thomas Hobbes writes (<u>Leviathon</u> II. In xix.95): "They that are displeased with Aristocracy, called it Oligarchy." But, before we go further, let us step back a notch in time, for this next small story is the linchpin to the argument. Without this relevant sally, we would miss the fulcrum or nexus of the issue.

Back in 1962 the country faced the prospect of a slight recession. U.S. Steel, then one of the largest corporations in the country, (back when we actually used to make things!) seized upon that time to institute a relatively small price increase. President John Kennedy: Well, he threw down his glove! He ordered two of the company's top executives into the Oval Office and scolded them heartedly, "How can you call yourselves decent Americans when your greedy actions may catalyze an ever deeper economic downturn?" He challenged them stoutly and scolded them mercilessly. This man was a flying Scotchman who cared about the other members of his crew, that is, all Americans, not just big shot executives. And, guess what, within days, the small price increase had been rescinded. And for Kennedy it had been a wingdinger of a day!

Remember, this man was the son of the beyond-clever Joseph P. Kennedy who pulled his money out of Wall Street just before the crash of 1929. This man, too, having seen how his father ruthlessly operated his financial affairs, as noted, said that all businessmen are bastards. Are they? One wonders, did he really think it so, or was he merely speaking for effect, trying to appear experienced beyond his 40-odd years, or, as we used to say, high, wide and handsome?

Why have I resurrected this four-decade-old example? What pertinence does it hold for us today? The answer is this: Back then the government told large financial entities what to do, instead of the other way around. Kennedy argued that for <u>the good of the entire country</u> the steel company's increase must be returned and with some hectoring, lecturing pressure Kennedy was acceded to. Undoubtedly, the same would not happen today and we must ask ourselves why that is. Why is our government so passive, so disinclined to attack, like General George McClellan <u>at and after</u> the battle at Antietam Creek? Why is there this shilly-shally unwillingness or inability on the part of government to control Wall Street? How did the Groupthinkers (Ostriches all!) at the Security and Exchange Commission not investigate Bernard Madoff's black-flagged Ponzi scheme, a dusty and gross gimmick if there ever were one, despite repeated (14?) complaints from countless corners? In short, where are the gimlet-eyed agents, those keen, mean, and sharp-sighted enough to control or rein in the gilded youths, the rogues, the treacherous and profligate, or the merely wanton?

The quick response is we have set up a revolving door between the government and the eager beavers at the banks. It spins and never stops! Routinely, corruptly, collusively, workers at one retire and begin employment the next day at the other. Goldman Sachs is called, not always derisively, Government Sachs. A Royal We emerges, playing a "sport royal,"[5] and they slip in from the private to the public sector, changing jobs from one side of the fence to the other as deftly as they change a rumpled, Sea Island cotton shirt for a fresh one. It is no wonder, given this unclean and lazy predicament, that the agile MBAer, bouncing so blithely back and forth, is privy to closely held, august information which he withholds or retains for possible, self-aggrandizing use later on. Secrets are passed on quietly within this exclusive club, this small circle of ogog elites. Transparency is long past, or considered not rascally enough. Recondite maneuvers perpetuate, hidden from view or the scorching glare of the sun. The press is mostly silent or unaware. Furtiveness abounds, and government has lost any stringent force, sapped dry and dull by these growing, reckless entanglements. Willy-nilly, we have thus established a gang of privied elites, a circle of financial friends who control our dollars' destiny. A given individual on the outside will make massive, mostly unearned amounts of money at a bank, and

5   William Shakespeare. <u>Twelfth Night</u> (II.3. 171)

then, as he chooses, step into government to make policy: He is thus getting his bread buttered on two sides, yet no one seems to object. Where is the populist uproar? Where were the pulsating protests when three billion dollars of the forty-five billion loaned to <u>both</u> Citibank and Bank of America were used to pay out extravagant bonuses to the top managers? Did not the government know and expect that those bonuses were to be paid out of taxpayers' funds? All of these events could only have happened if collusion, pervasive and at the highest levels, existed within the oligarchy.

Of course, all of these happenings are entirely our fault, since, sleepily, we allowed these invalid and nefarious conditions to breed and flourish. The Big Club, as I term it, whose members are as independent as hogs on ice, was formed by our own lassitude and silence. It is our own stupid fault! So, it must be dismantled piece by piece, part by part, since the present course is completely untenable: Our current economic condition must not persist. A full and vigorous reform must be joined. The lot of more than the members of the Big Club must be made, once again, predominate. It shall not be quick or easy battle and we must steal ourselves for a long and nasty fight, yet unless we now join this struggle against this collusive financial oligarchy, the prince and the police poised together, it will coerce and attract even more unfair windfalls to come their way. If we do nothing or not enough, if we do not complete the job entirely, I fear that our democracy, even though one filled with far more little men than large ones, will continue to slip away until its last slim vestiges attenuate and finally disappear.

Who is there to say, "No!" to the banks? Who among us may raise a strident voice to dare to call out the obvious: Financial institutions have gone too far? Who might ask what the Founding Fathers might think of this gilded mess? Who may speak again of the story of Midas, now long neglected? Who will posit that in business there is no room for falsehoods or for secrets? Who does not know the difference between mine and thine? Who will argue the obvious point that the "heads I win, tails you lose" mentality must cease?

Unless this conflict is joined and until it is won, our country will remain rudderless and lost, her ship showing a flag of distress and her peoples poorly served by delirious captains who have sadly lost their way. Maybe we should recall Captain George Washington DeLong (1844-1881) who sailed the Jeanette towards the North Pole. She became caught in ice and drifted for 21 months. Eventually Captain DeLong starved to death. (The Dictionary of Nautical Literacy. Robert McKenna. International Mariners. McGraw Hill: Comden, Maine. 2001. P. 97)

Young Turks: Any group of young or relatively young men full of new ideas and impatient for change.

Well, thus we play the fools with the time, and the spirits of the wise sit in the clouds and mock us.

William Shakespeare
<u>King</u> <u>Henry</u> <u>IV</u>. Part II. Act II. Scene 2. Line 135

President Calvin, "Silent Cal" Coolidge, was a benign presence in the White House, content to let the bankers, industries and speculators run the country as they saw fit.

Tom Brokaw
<u>The</u> <u>Greatest</u> <u>Generation</u>. New York: Random House. 1998. P.4

Chapter Two:
Old Turks Versus Young Turks

Please join with me then: May we not have some segway way, tooting fun?

Old-fashioned bankers, the cautioning types that pretty much do not exist anymore, remind me of <u>The Catcher Who Was a Spy</u>[6], Moe Berg. That portly catcher and linguist owned just one black suit, a dozen white-only shirts and a single black tie. He must have looked like a non-smiling mortician whenever he visited Joe Dimaggio at the Waldorf-Astoria and stayed for days.

Similarly, bankers of my father's age might have had two navy suits, and, then, perhaps, one grey one, for the more social gatherings, and they would have been made of either wool flannel or serge: No sharkskin, glen plaids or elaborate overlays, ever. Do you hear? The maker might have been Brooks Brothers but not their fancy Golden Fleece line since that one was too pricey and not worth the extra money.

---

6   Dawidoff, Nicholas. <u>The Catcher Who Was a Spy</u>: <u>The Mysterious Life of Moe Berg</u>. New York: Pantheon Books, 1994.

Dominic M. Martin

Indeed, back then, many office types would have preferred to purchase a suit with two pairs of trousers (as they called them then), since, as everyone knows (or ought to), it is the trousers that wear out first, particularly at the bottom and cuff, and that way, too, the wearer could switch pants every other day, allowing one pair of trousers to rest and air out and its creases to smooth themselves away.

Today, I both suspect and know, the wardrobe of a banker is considerably more extensive. Prince of Wales plaids are common. All manner of fabrics and pattern are seen. Variety is key. Clever clothing advisers are sought out for keen advice on what sort of suit best matches one's skin tone or the eyes. A banker must not wear the same suit two days in a row since that would create the obvious impression that he is dowdy or a seedy toad. To complete the fresh look of the togs, shoes must match, whether in finish bookbinder, cardovan, or brogue, and the braces, too, must be coordinated within the entire outfit, so that one clear impression is given, to the boss or client, that of manliness, determination, and a vibrant force.

Yet, why this silly, happy as Harry, diversion? Selah. A pause, our first, is another rare word from <u>Brewer's</u>[7], p. 1010. <u>Brewer's</u> is quoted often throughout these pages because it is detailed, idiosyncratic, eccentric; it is filled with thousands of bits of arcane knowledge. Through the inclusion of <u>Brewer's</u>, I try to suggest that the world is hard, not easy, to perceive with clarity. It is complicated and layered, complicated and layered. It, therefore, brushes up against the limits of language and knowledge, and, correspondingly, its presence in the world and here suggests the necessary tension between humility (I am foolish) and arrogance (I am not foolish). Were not the bankers excessively confident

7   <u>Brewer's</u> <u>Dictionary</u> of <u>Phrase</u> <u>and</u> <u>Fable</u> Revised Edition by
    Ivor H. Evans; London: Cassell Ltd, 1988.

in their knowledge? Are they not still? Why does one have to re-read <u>Brewer's</u>? Should not one good and thorough reading of it be enough? Do you mean to say that I soon can forget or that I do not know everything? But, like, Mercury, I go too fast and steal some from the future. He is the god of rogues, vagabonds and thieves (<u>Brewer's</u> p. 729) To these lofty issues, we shall return, but only after the ground floor had been solidly built by a proper carpenter's hands. St. Joseph, pray for us.

To return to our discussion of clothes, Shakespeare gives us a leading clue to his fascination with mien. In <u>King Lear</u>, he writes:

> Through tatter'd clothes small vices do appear;
> Robes and furr'd gowns hide all.
>> William Shakespeare. <u>King Lear</u>. Act
>> IV. Scene 6. Line 164

Which is to say that bankers, like clowns or priests, butchers or painters, don the navy blue since it is a camouflage, this uniform, and if one of them, or more, is evil, it will not be noticed:

> And thus I clothe my naked villainy With odd old ends stolen forth of Holy Writ And seem a saint when most I play the devil.
>> William Shakespeare. <u>King Richard III</u>. Act I, Scene 3, Line 336

Staunching, now, the flood of words on cloth, whether stammel of dullest red or Zegna's high performance weave, how do these men, these young Turks, act? Are they descended at all from their fathers, the old stodgy ones, like mine, or are they cut from separate cloth; are they of careless or carefree bearing, and to whose standard do they adhere? Hessian's? Soldiers of fortune? Baruch?

I maintain that today most bankers are a separate breed; they are altered fully from their monetary forebears. They eschew caution. Their first thought is not of their client, but of the bank. They have no more in common with the old-fashioned prudent bankers of the 50's than I do with whales or ducks. Technology gains their every move, yet, behind that, they think, as masterminds, as gamblers, differently: They regard the world with eager vision and see risk as a friend, as something to be used, or hedged, always in their favor. Everything, or so they arrogantly thought before Humpty-Dumpty (Brewer's, p. 576) came crashing down, is manageable or can be mitigated. Such is the level of their hubris (Still! That word again!) that they continue to produce foul smelling, galling statements of the future which they deem to control. Bad sausage or tripe.

Some, the worst, are outright deceivers, nasty flatterers intending to lull suspicion to better work their mischief. Brewer's calls it "To carry food in one hand and water in the other. That is to say one thing and mean another." (p. 201) Thus, a new way of false speaking has emerged. And, at the higher reaches many executives surround themselves with sycophants, and flatterers, who if they possess independent thoughts, do not speak them.

On the other hand, some young Turks are tops! Some, the best, are copies of their fathers: Avoiding risk, urging caution, not talking advantage. They try, whenever possible, to build real, non-ethereal wealth, not to churn or skim for a quick profit. My innate familial bias tells to me that they tend to be clustered in the Midwest and always in smaller towns[8]. Such a blanketing generality cannot be proven. I do know that this more cautionary segment is vastly outnumbered, and maybe going the way of the dodo bird or phone prefixes, that is to say, extinct!

Most foolishly, banks may give money to political candidates, and, when those candidates become elected, the banks will them tell them what to do and how to do it. This is cunning and duplicitous behavior, suggesting the currying of favor (Brewer's, p. 301) that Shakespeare in The Merchant of Venice writes of:

> The seeming truth which cunning times put on to entrap the wisest.
>
> III.2.100

By their frank acceptance of these filthy funds, ugly pelf, these congressmen, ensconced in the regal halls of power, rarely ready to be dislodged, they have become unwitting accomplices to corruption. Once the lawmaker's independence (the ability to tell someone to cram it!) is gone, all rub or impediment to the banks is likewise deported. So describes our nation.

Therefore, presidents of both parties have actually helped to deregulate Wall Street, encouraging hedge funds, derivatives, credit default swaps, programmed and block trading, short selling, mortgage backed securities, overnight turns, and loans to homeowners who do not have anywhere near the requisite cash flow. All of these things are either intrinsically destabilizing or can only benefit the institutional investor, not the average Joe. Constantly, they and Congress looked the other way when a parson's close attention should have been paid. Some of these devil-may-

---

8 (E.g.) Feldman & Stern, who wrote Too Big to Fail are from Minnesota, just like my pop!)

care entities were put in place by the banks or financial institutions themselves and the SEC or the Federal Reserve, which should have severely questioned them or (God forbid!) Said "No!", just looked the other way, frozen, fearful, facing downward, perhaps examining the ground for slugs or snails. Progressively, Wall Street over the last 30 years has become more and more salacious (yes: Lust!) and dangerous, a lion's den; yet, for awhile, especially in the 90's, financial profits were astronomical which, of course, led to <u>even</u> <u>greater</u> de-regulation and risk-taking. Consequently, Wall Street had placed itself precariously on chaos' edge and the president, all presidents, have only fiddled while Rome burned.

Risk is the new mantra: Are you manly enough? Is there enough testosterone in the room or should we get another shot? Take a leap! I can promise more than you! The Romans had an apt phrase, "Barba tenus sapientes," literally 'wise as far as the beard,' i.e., with the appearance of wisdom only. Yet, were not the normal American people supremely conned by these "city slickers," those "glib, clever, socially adroit . . . smoothies who achieves success by being well-liked and personable."[9]

Am I too harsh, too generalizing, too arch? Do I overstate the case against the bankers? No. Why? Proof?: Under the bankers' inept aegis, Wall Street lost 40% of its value in 2008. Wealth was halved and fortunes lost. Homes were foreclosed upon and precious assets sold in a down market, further confirming losses, just to buy milk. Children continue to need milk.

All the president cut no ice. They have had and plan no drastic reform. They merely watch as hedge funds, which did not exist 30 years and whose pull out of Bear Stearns acted

---

9   <u>Dictionary</u> <u>of</u> <u>American</u> <u>Slang</u>. Wentworth and Flexner. Thomas Y. Crowell Company: New York, NY, 1975. P. 487.

as the meltdown's catalyst, continue to proliferate. They are not the wise guardians at the gate, as they purport to be, nor hunters of risk and rascals. They play a mean double game, holding with the hare and running with the hounds, that is "playing a double game, trying to keep in touch with both sides."[10] Their job is to protect all the American people, but since they all have taken the money, ok vast sums of monies (Thank you, Mr. David Mamet) from the financial institutions, they, too, have inherently, and instantly lost all independence. They are no longer one of "The Untouchables." Once bankers give to any president funds they can and do tell him what to do and, more importantly, what not to do. Therefore, he gazes out the window and sees no harm. Golf? Tennis? Only years of collusion at the oligarchy could have made this distressing scene possible.

When we first spoke with the Bank years ago, none of this was discussed. All the focus was on long term investing in solid companies, holding under-valued stocks for many years, patiently waiting for proper appreciation and decent profit. These experts, so-called, did not see the technology bubble about to burst, nor the debacle of 2008. Consequently, they were not the experts that they purported to be. Though they looked the part, dressed in the finest Brioni suit with expensive matching scarpe, they were overpaid masquerades, reckless, feckless, gambling with other's money, and, of course, planning to suffer no real losses of their own. To conclude, we must recall Aesop's words:

> The lamb that belonged to the sheep, whose skin the wolf was wearing, began to follow the wolf in the sheep's clothing... Appearances are deceiving.
> Aesop. The Wolf in Sheep's Clothing.

10   Brewer's, p.530

Oh, to return to the old days, when a man owned 1 or 2 suits only, like Moe Berg did, and a fellow knew that when a banker said something to you, it <u>had</u> to be true. Had to be. There would be no doubt as to his prudent accuracy. Then, they were as predictable as swallows returning to Mission San Juan Capistrano, since the last thing that any of them would ever want to do would be to lead someone down the wrong path.

To be honest, as this world goes, is to be one man picked out of ten thousand.

William Shakespeare, <u>Hamlet</u>
Act II, Scene 2, Line 178

Not greedy of filthy lucre

I Timothy. III, 3.

Go to now, ye rich men, weep and howl for your miseries that should come upon you. Your riches are corrupted and your garments are moth-eaten. Your gold and silver is cankered; and the rust of them shall be a witness against you, and shall eat your flesh as if it were fire.

James 5: 1-3

Chapter Three:
On Capitalism, or the Toaster

A few years ago, we had a small accident on our kitchen stove and scorched the bottom of our Krups teakettle so badly that it had to be tossed into the tip. Wanting to replace it, we repurchased the same model and, while opening the box, I noticed that this new kettle had been made in China, the securing nation, by the way, of most of our country's burgeoning debt. This made me ask myself: Why can we not make, apparently, a toaster here? Rising and excessive union wages, especially in the Northeast and Midwest, led to the passage of the North American Free Trade Agreement (NAFTA) which, more than anything else, in turn, led to the construction of hundreds of factories in Mexico, just beyond our 1300 mile long border with that country. The people working in those factories work for considerably less than the Yankees and, thus, the final product, usually meant to be sold in the United States, is much less expensive than it would have been, had it been manufactured north of the Rio Grande. Unsurprisingly, a gigantic loss of manufacturing jobs has taken place here and, thus, we have become, almost overnight, largely a service economy.

On an annual golf trip (5 days, 10 rounds, no wives, much beer!) I recall arguing about this own-created, foozled predicament with my cronies. So steadfast was, and is, our friendship that, even though it was 3 guys to 1, I never felt surrounded! They argued that we should all be afforded the chance to purchase a toaster at a lower price, that that was capitalism at its best, and that to attempt to curtail the normal marketing of cheaper goods would be a harmful restraint of trade. I rejoined that the loss of manufacturing jobs would have unforecastable and far-reaching consequences and that I would not mind paying $200 instead of $50 for a toaster as long as it was of vastly superior quality and durability. Finally, I screeched, reaching for another beer, "We can't all work in the service sector!" They looked at me badly and said, plaintively, "Why not?," and just there, so obliquely, the short debate derailed.

If I had had more of my mean wit about me, and not just various containers of malted beverage, I might have proposed for their deserved consideration the following interlaced ideas: That someone who builds a toaster factor, or a lamp factory, or a winery, must gather together all the "foodstuff for the sandwich," that is, all the parts and raw materials must be sourced, paid for, and shipped to the factory where, with deft design and artistry, something more beautiful and utilitarian, like a toaster, is produced. A toaster is a thing of greater value than its disparate and unassembled parts, and, in fact, a <u>modicum</u> of new wealth has been created. It was on this splendid basis that the cumulative wealth of the United States grew so exponentially during and after World War II. Clearly, the service industry for its part, does not engender this "Value Added" factor, a problematic circumstance not sufficiently considered in our nation's hasty retreat from manufacturing and our correspondent embrace of the service side.

Thus, brownfields have emerged, and more, further rusted; shuttered factories are everywhere. Near where we live, the once-industrious Mohawk Valley, its manufacturing plants long closed, lies fallow. Dozens of towns have lost most of their population, and those people that remain there often wish to leave, but cannot afford to do so. Every two or four years, politicians running for office make the profane, if not laughable, boast that they will bring jobs back to the Mohawk, but such empty claims are no more than self-serving babble, bunk. I do not know why someone in the complaisant, eager-to-be-lied-to crowd does not raise a fervid voice to ask the most important question, always, which is: "How?"

This sharp decrease in the number of manufacturing jobs has handed the service industry, but especially the halfbacks of the financial industry an open field on which to expand, run. In my non-proletarian view, the growth of the financial industry has been excessive. May I say so? As an economy, we all are better off with a much greater balance among the various sectors, and I believe that this fact, in our headlong rush to get rid of manufacturing, was, also, never sufficiently studied. Without a vibrant manufacturing sector, that needed balance may not exist, however much we may wish it so. We are all better served if there is a more than nascent competition among the various sectors. When manufacturing faltered, when the toaster business moved to China or Mexico or wherever else it moved to in search of always lower labor costs, the financial industry ballooned in its place; and that ballooning, I maintain, has been harmful to our country. All the various segments in any nation's economy ought to be roughly in balance or else the entire country will suffer when one grows too large.

When financial profits are seen as a percentage of overall U.S. business profits, in 1950, that percentage was a reasonable 8%; in 2007, that number had climbed, unreasonably, to 27%. (For further discussion of low financial profits, as a percentage of GNP, can be excessive, read James Crotty's article in the Cambridge Journal of Economic entitled "Structural Causes of the Global Financial Crisis: A Critical Assessment of the New Financial Architecture" 2009 Vol 33, #4, p. 563-580.) Thus, essentially, a financial oligarchy has been formed whereby a few powerful entities largely run the country's economy. It used to be that the government told the financial industry what to do. Now, as a general rule, no longer. As Simon Johnson, the well-known MIT economist says: financial institutions have "sewn up power as surely as any Banana Republic". [11]

We have seen the 2008 meltdown, families pommeled, fortunes eviscerated, yet where are the strong-willed attempts at real reform? It's nowhere to be seen since the too-powerful banks fight any resurgent attempt by government for greater control. Here is the rubric: Nouriel Roubini's remark "Recovery will fail unless we break apart the financial oligarchy which is blocking essential reform."[12] He is called Dr. Doom only by those that stand to suffer should his populist notions be adopted.

Many years ago, graduates of the venerable Ivy League schools scattered widely across the nation to work for all sectors of industry. Yet, today, once again and unhappily, 40% of the graduates, lured by outstanding salaries and ludicrous

11 From "On Point" with Tom Ashbrook March 31, 2009 "Are the Banks Running America?"
12 Nouriel Roubini. New York University Professor of Economics Huffington Post April 4, 2009

year-end bonuses, immediately work in Wall Street. I call them the "blue suits," perhaps a bit too derisively. Because of the 2008 meltdown, that percentage may shortly decline. However, here, two quick points need to be made.

The first is another one made many years ago by my always jawing, wise father. Examining the sharp increase in jobs at Wall Street in the 1970's, he whispered to me, in what I first took to be an incongruous or profane aside, "There are too many guys on the boob!", meaning that the financial industry employs, wastefully, too many people, or so I correctly figured after a turn of head scratching. The cost of all those jobs must, of course, be paid for before the bank's profit, which, in turn, must mean higher fees to be garnered from the Average Joe.

And the second, equally salient fact is this: If, instead of the number of 40%, that is, if a greater percentage of graduates (like in the old days!) went to work for that factory, yes, indeed, perhaps that toaster factory, just perhaps, with their brains and much old-fashioned American common sense (using one's "g.d. noodle" as my dad used to say), it might have been resurrected or saved. Let us imagine again a nation wherein toasters, Phoenix-like, are still made in Toledo or Sandusky: Think of all the seen and unseen benefits which would, by necessity, accrue. Consider that the toaster might probably be more solid, and last longer. And ponder that the financial world would not have become so monolithic, and, therefore, so likely to dominate.

I say all these things, which may appear at first blush as likely the comments of a neo-Bolshevist, instead as the comments of a stubborn capitalist and the son of an archetypal, i.e., cautious banker, who would know, if he were alive, that the financial institutions have become far too powerful and overreaching, with scant meaningful regulation or control from a compliant government.

I knew that NAFTA was an intrinsic mistake the first time I heard about it, how it had to be an awful bane to factories here. Disgraceful! Pickpockets! Lackeys! I remember H. Ross Perot's quick and accurate retort:

"There will be a giant sucking sound,"
the sound of jobs disappearing from the U.S.A. Why was he the only one sharp eyed? Many Midwestern states, especially Ohio, Michigan and Pennsylvania have been hit particularly hard, and (what do you know!) those are the same states that today are having a very difficult time paying their bills. Who would have ever thunk it, Miriam? Did anyone consider the probable and sizeable loss of payroll tax to the state's revenues, Ethel? Why were we in such a damn and giggly hurry to sign that stupid bill, Bill? Did Big Business put pressure on President Clinton to pass this flawed legislation which, surely, could only result in huge losses of jobs in this country? If so, why did he not tell them to "pound sand?" Does not the president represent all Americans, not just the rich, powerful, or well-connected?

Assuredly, money is at the root of the problem: If a president has not taken any funds from Big Business (banks or whomever), he thereby retains the independence of thought necessary to be able to say "Scram!" or "Shoo!" to someone whose idea, he thinks, is bunk or drivel. The fact that President Clinton signed NAFTA and also bills de-regulating the financial institutions means that, not only was there back in the early 90's, collusion at the oligarchy but that it was pretty thick!

Yes, other factors are at work, especially those at the unions. I allege that for years they were too strong, that they pushed for and received wages that were simply untenable, thus forcing management to look elsewhere (Mexico, China, Macau...) for a shot at greater profitability. But, I ask: Should a guy bolting on a bumper really make more than $40 per hour? It must be argued that excessive union wage demands played a large role in forcing manufacturing out of the country.

So, lucky stars! Today, Levi Strauss, Merrill, Converse are made, mostly, somewhere else. Terrific! As a kid, my mom bought me Converse tennis shoes or "sneakers," as we used to call them, made in Massachusetts. They were pretty heavy, made of stiff think canvas and real rubber. At first, if you did not wear thick socks, they would give you mean, super-duper blisters! But, if your feet did not outgrow them, they would last for years! Now they are not as tough. Are we better off?

Too, I remember Hathaway shirts, and especially the advertisement where the guy with one black eye patch, and with a nice plaid shirt on, always got the girl, a lissome, nice one. (Such teeth!: Sorry, my dandy rises) Over time, with rising wage costs and the inability to raise prices much, the Hathaway shirt factory in Maine closed. Four times the town (Waterville?) tried to resurrect, again like Phoenix, the business, and four times it failed to do so. Today the space is occupied by restaurants and architecture offices: Skimble-skamble.

Maybe, as a country we would be better off if we were willing to pay just a little more for a product if it were made in the United States. Take, for example, a pair of Merrill boots: If they are rugged, made here, yet cost $100, instead of $75, could an American not buy them anyway, thinking they might last longer due to higher quality? He could also assume that he is helping to preserve American jobs, albeit in a very small way. The volumetric flask fills by the smallest, unseen increments.

I, a dolt, conclude, with a jolt, on a bolt, yes, a bolt! The other way I noted that out younger daughter's toy red wagon needed a paint job. I had some Lawn Green paint (Yes, different, but: Why not, Gracie?), so we, the scamp and I, set to work. Then, she mentioned that a brace had come loose, and I saw that at its terminus a bolt and nut were affixed there, hard and frozen, rusted together. They would have to be cut off from the brace, but how?

But, what a job! It took nearly an hour, using vice grips, all manner of pliers, and, finally, a hack saw and a table vice. The bolt was tough as nails! Hard as cider! Half-way through the job, cursing, spitting, flailing, I realized that the wagon was an old one, that the bolt had a higher iron content than today's version from China would have, and that the wagon must have been made here in the U.S.A. Can we not return, a little, to those halcyon days? Will I be labeled a racist if I allege that the Chinese quality of manufacture is nowhere near what our's used to be?

I remember my toys as a kid: They were heavy and rugged, and my bike's chrome lasted, gleamed. My baseball glove (sadly, gone) was a Rawlings and it was, of course, made here. Almost everything I had - clothes, bikes, games, toys - was made in America. I recall how much like cardboard my Levi Strauss jeans were when I first brought them home from the store. It took many months to get the heavy stiffness out. My Penny's white T-shirts were woven tightly like serge, and my Pendleton wool shirts were dense and thick with considerable body and texture. Nearly everything spoke to quality, excellence, and durability!

In the name of profit, most of that has changed. Nearly all of our children's clothes is made offshore and it is thin and shoddy. They are cheap and cheaply made, not meant to last, so they don't. Just the other day, our son told me that his brand-new down coat was "breezy." The word is SCHLOCK!, something cheaply made of inferior material, design and workmanship. Interestingly, at least to me, the word, schlock is from the Yiddish for some word meaning "a curse."

Even worse is the endless proliferation of kids' second-rate, schlub electronic gadgets, all of which, of course, did not exist back in my day. The very great majority is junk and will be ending up in landfills quickly enough, where the sulfuric acid in the batteries will eventually leach out into the groundwater, but, that is, Manfred, another story.

To anticipate: Yes, I understand the strong global forces allied against us in any nascent or proposed rebirth of manufacturing, and they are many and daunting. But did not W.H. Auden say, "People are meant to produce things?" We must be clever and resourceful, and to use all our wits and not just some. If we don't, our nation's economic ship will continue to drift about, perhaps taking on water, about to founder. Secondarily, would it not be a happy circumstance for the overly expanded financial institutions, having now grown to unbridled, Herculean strength, to have, at last, some stiffening competition?

Heaven is above all yet; there sits a judge That no
king can corrupt
> William Shakespeare
> <u>King</u> <u>Henry</u> <u>VIII</u>. Act III, Scene I,
> Line 99.

If you can walk three miles, you can walk four.
> Luis Aromijo's father.
> Quoted by Tom Brokaw in his book,
> <u>The</u> <u>Greatest</u> <u>Generation</u>. New York:
> Random House, 1998: p. 206

But it's our wits that make us men.
> Anderson, Lin. <u>Braveheart.</u> [Video]
> Prod. Icon Productions, 1995.

Chapter Four:
Letter to a Wise Chinese Doctor

At some point during the meteoric rise of the financial industry's ascension to the highest reaches, climbing that most dangerous of Matterhorns, it became fashionable, if not expected, for a bank, being so steadily successful, so awash in cash, to hire a think-thank expert or ersatz shepherd to guard the blue-suited flock against any incipient or unseen dangers. No: That is not quite true — a given bank would not hire one shepherd but dozens of them, and they would work in delegated teams with carefully separated areas of responsibility, that carving-up of effort designed to maximize effectiveness and eliminate all redundancies. They were hired by the bank to protect it from all untoward losses, and to plan for a glorious and unsoiled future. So: Is it not now correct or fortuitous to ask whether they, these acknowledged and heavily schooled experts, did their jobs? Was excellence achieved or averted? Or are all answers to these questions moot and unwanted? Are all such shirty (re: <u>Brewer's</u>: "Bad-tempered, very cross and offended." P. 1027) questions profitless?

Before proceeding, I must dally again some short distance. Please excuse. While studying wine making and grape growing in college over 30 years ago (small voices of moaning emerge, tentative cries of appointed alarm, and consternation, mews, of a dotty harmed by the aging's endless cyclic march), I was assigned, not unpleasantly, to take a 4-month course on "Steam, its Uses and Justifications," and upon entering the classroom two of my compatriots who, like myself, happened to be white males (all three of us with already growing paunches and already slipping libidos), there, the three of us were surprised to see that our fellow students, some two score or thereabouts, were uniformly Asian females, once again, not unhappily to our always wandering eyes, since so pleasing were their slender forms and so beguiling their eager eyes. Was I about to be transfixed by such beauteous faces, or had the seduction happened already? Already I knew that during the term my mind would endlessly drift, endlessly drift, as a ship might upon the wide Sargasso Sea. Would the three of us not get caught up in that abundant sea, or simply lost and confused upon her calm and limitless waters? Already, too, I felt myself meek and foolish before their transcending intelligence. And, the funny thing is this — where mirth, once again, becomes a feast and all manner of jokes are abounding, in festive play and with no derision — that the professor came over to we three blanchers (another white male, but older and, if I recall correctly, from the Buckeye state of Ohio) and said, like Marx might, to us, "Well, gentleman, there goes the curve!" Such a cute, wry comment could only have been uttered before Political Correctness became, ipso facto, the law of the land. Was he not unshyly implying that those lovely young ladies would most probably get the As and that we could be fortunate to manage meager Bs? How rash! Was he not attesting to their greater intrinsic brain power and security of thought, especially as it relates to scientific issues? And, in so doing, was he not properly exercising his First Amendment rights of free speech? Is it not also true that if he were to make that some statement in a classroom today that he would be roundly admonished as a traducer? If so, what has altered or changed so utterly? Has the public consciousness of what is proper so fully molted? What was the unseen catalyst to that shedding of a past's unmean monument to what is right? Who is it that has made these new rules? (That question is at the foundation of this book.) What force of authority will make sure that they will be adhered to? And, most crucially, how will we know if they will work? By the by, the professor was absolutely correct: Nearly all the beauteous Asian females received the As, and I and my few fawning white boys limped home with grades in the lower B range. "Oh, Doctor!" as Ruzzuto, the scooter, might have said. He had knocked us down a peg, but it did not matter much to me and the others because he was right.

* * *

The following 3 letters were written to a brilliant female doctor of finance, one of Asian extraction (Chinese, Korean: Who is to say?) and bountiful intelligence. They were written as the financial tsunami most acutely and quickly hit our family, one of many millions equally hard hit, (Brewer's defines "hard-hit" as badly affected, especially by monetary losses." We also know the phrase "hard-up," meaning short of money; and, too, can recall the film from Evelyn Waugh's Brideshead Revisited wherein Charles Ryder's father lectures his son on the dozens of similar terms, including: "Tight, hard done by, on the rocks, and bereft." p. 529) and they, therefore, reflect no small measure of anguish and fear, anger and fright.

Perhaps smartly, she deigned to not respond; after all, if she had chosen to answer letters such as these, ones so trifling, so insignificant, so daft, so unanswerable, all the other ones sent to her, those similar in mocking tone and unmasked derision, they would equally have necessitated her response. And if that had been done, what else more propitious, would have been left unaccomplished, undone? What greater deed left unfinished, what other, less mean task disused?

Then derisive, I today feel the more kindly towards her. Accordingly, I now regret these letters' caustic tone, their stridency and short belittlements, yet that regret changes less their form since they are fixed, immutable, or cast in stone. They have been both sent and received.

Strangely, still, across the country, I feel her friendship. As things are, she wishes to speak, but cannot: Her male bosses would disapprove of it. I understand that she may never go counter to their wishes. In this, her submissiveness, she rises still higher in my fancy. At length, then, more and more, she becomes my friend. She, in time, transmutes, under my cautious begging, into a "herdsman, careful of his herd" (Joyce); and eventually, under the luxuriant prodding of the imagination, one undeterred and little steered, I know that once, long ago, before the cymbals or the bellows, we had met. Over 30 years ago, I now know that the two of us had gathered in a classroom together, both of us, to study steam. Long before either one of us had earned even one Krone or Lira. Of course, she would have received an A! Of course! The highest grade possible! How could it even have been otherwise! She was brilliant then, just as she is brilliant now! Her parents would have been most proud of her transcending intelligence. Always, she did not wise to disappoint them. Always, too, that professor had been right, even though politically incorrect: Asians <u>are</u> smarter. Why may he not now so speak again? Why can't we let loose his wayward tongue?

Dear Dr. Peek Woo,

The purpose of this note is to make a kind and pointed personal appeal: We need your help.

Since the late 50s when I used to deposit checks at the Manhattan Beach, California, Bank of _____ for my father's business and on to today, nearly all of my banking business has been with your bank. My mother, now long deceased, once had a friendship with one of the bank's founder's wives. Yet, lately, because of 3 margin calls in the last 60 days, that loyalty has been tested.

Back in 2001, the Bank lost a fortune for us due to a severe dip in the market. In the last 2 months the same sort of losses have occurred. Day traders have taken over the market, resulting in huge and costly swings. Fancy derivative products have been invented, though few can explain what they are or how they work. Thousands of hedge funds have been instituted which also increase the market's instability: When Lehman Brothers folded, a hedge fund divest was at the core. Finally, poor oversight allowed Freddie and Fannie to make poor, politically motivated loans to people who should probably rent. But, what has all of this to do with you and our relationship?

Because of the aforementioned conditions, we have not, so far, been able to sell our Vermont house; upon a sale, which we 17 months ago had every reason to expect, those funds would have been entirely applied to the line-of-credit, those avoiding the 3 margin calls. Those 3 margin calls only confirmed losses, making our financial condition even more precarious. Why was there not some consideration given to the considerable value of our Tupper Lake home. These margin calls, ma'am, though legal, were unethical, and I know that my father, long deceased and also a banker, would agree. Banks are supposed to help people, not bully them in

31

the middle of a perfect storm, as has taken place here. These times demand <u>new</u>, <u>keen</u> solutions.

Do you not feel some sort of responsibility regarding the huge losses that we have suffered? Over the 10 years of our investment with the Bank, the rate of return has been abysmal: All forecasts have fallen short. Like many, because of the "fast and loose" climate of Wall Street which you and many others either encouraged or allowed to happen, I no longer believe that it is a good place to put one's money. That could change but, first, hedge funds, derivative packages and programmed day-trading would have to disappear and that is something that most bankers, even after this debacle, which has affected the "little guy" more that the big shot, would not like to forsake.

Here is what we want: 1) a calculation made regarding how much the 3 margin calls cost us and a paydown of the line-of-credit by that same amount. 2) An elimination of all bank fees until the Dow returns to 12,750. 3) More attention paid to my IRA which was at "x" and whose value today I do not wish to study. This is probably the 10th time I have made this request, but, since few at your end seem to listen, I must go directly to you.

Absent these changes we will have to sell the Tupper Lake house in a down market, pay off all debt and leave the Bank for friendlier climes. Please do not make us do that.

My father was in the Navy, and my uncle 22 years in the Marines. I was raised with a few core ideas: Pay attention to the details, finish the job and admit your mistakes. Don't defend yourself and don't criticize others. Maybe some of your team need to be taught these lessons anew.

Drastic times in the middle of a perfect storm require new and courageous measures. Our small mistakes do not warrant your punitive, if not confiscatory, actions. Our family puts their faith in your kind and fair judgement in the hope that some improvement, favorable to us both, may be secured.

Sincerely,

Dominic Martin

11/4/2008

PS. I have a better and different idea, change #4: Calculate all fees collected for the year 2008 and remit against the line-of-credit. These fees were not earned, but only computer generated. Perhaps our account manager, Mr. Daniel Lord, who a month ago suggested that I am stupid, would be happy to match those funds personally. I may be irritating and occasionally bombastic, but I am not stupid. He owes us and you an apology. By the way, what about this idea: The bank does not collect fees of any sort unless it generates a profit?

Dear Dr. Peek Woo:

It is now even more clear, given the 50 Billion dollar Madoff Ponzi scheme announced the other day, that the stock market as a whole is awash in corruption: That is, many that work there, labor only for their own narrow benefit, churning some small esoteric angle most vigorously for a huge and massively disproportionate financial gain. Madoff was busted by his own sons, pointing out how poor the government's regulatory ability is. This is one more example (not that we needed it!) proving that Wall Street has:

1) too many latched onto its edges, creaming obscene profits and doing <u>nothing</u> for our country, and

2) become a child's playpen for all manner of new, untested and unreliable financial entitities which must be gotten rid of if the American investor of average, not enormous wealth would wish to return to it.

To wit:

1) Hedge funds must be abolished
2) Day Trading must be abolished
3) Programmed block trading must be abolished
4) Derivatives must be abolished
5) International investors can only sell American-based stocks if they leave behind 5% upon a sale, that is, if it is commenced within 1 year of purchase.

Let us assume that the government cannot regulate the stock market; therefore, the market must regulate itself, something it is not wont to do. Christopher Cox, as head of the SEC, should have been fired 1 year ago. He is a symptom of the problem: Too much <u>cronyism</u>, which says that I will scratch your back if you scratch mine. The American people, not the financial types, know this and it is one of many reasons why they look askance at the 787 Billion Dollar Bail-out. "Fraud!," they cry, though their voice is not listened to in many of your elevated quarters.

The other main problem, which few seem to be discussing, is this: Loans should not be sold, packaged, re-sold, etc., but rather <u>kept</u> <u>by</u> <u>the</u> <u>bank</u> <u>that</u> <u>first</u> <u>made</u> <u>them</u>. What a modest proposal, Dr. Woo! Did you hear the National Public Radio story about the banker and the Amish people? He is making money! He would no more think about selling his loans to the Amish off to another bank than he would loan out his wife! A side benefit of this move would be a huge decrease in payroll which I read, is something that the Bank needs to be doing. Finally, an elimination of loan packaging and selling off would eliminate the triangle. When the bank sells a loan to a third party, the following dangerous triangle is set-up: Today, the Bank is so "in bed with" the underwriters that it is losing its base business, the average American customer. The underwriters have too much leverage on the Bank; but who <u>gave</u> them that leverage? The Bank. There are plenty of loyal, barking dogs round, but they are saying the wrong things and hurting your future business in an unseen and very fundamental way.

Ten years ago we invested in the Bank expecting a reasonable rate of return and stability. Neither has taken place. You have the moral right and the financial duty to tell our family how this has happened.

Our estimate is this: The financial world is full of people who really ought to be in Las Vegas. These are not prudent investors, but gamblers! Whatever happened to the slow and cautious banker of my parents' generation who looked out for the long-term interest of his customer? They would have been wary of undue underwriter strength.

For fun, let us construct a syllogism wherein A + B = C

> A)   Experts in the financial world ought to be able to predict and, therefore, to avoid any sort of deep financial instability.

> B)   The United States has been hit by an unpredicted and deep period of financial instability.

> C)   We did not have financial experts working for us, though that posed as such. Empty blue suits.

Unless the Bank return to the basics as outlined above, your business will suffer since the American investor of average income no longer trusts it: Wall Street is <u>not</u> a safe place to put one's money. Our family has lost a fortune investing with the Bank in 10 years. Now, the only safe place is bonds. The wheeler-dealers have killed the Golden Goose! And, why? The only answer is: Greed.

How do I know so much? My father was a product of the Depression; he saw banks foreclose on people left and right! Is not the same thing happening today? I bet that you have a slew of over-paid consultants saying many of the same things I have just said. But from me, there is no charge!

But, please, get the underwriters off our back. My wife and I are trying vigorously to sell our 2 homes, at which point we will take the first proceeds to pay off the line-of-credit. We are giving up on "dream home" in favor of a greater fiscal certainty. By giving us some time, will you not help us?

Sincerely,

Dominic

Dear Dr. Peek Woo: 12/17/08

Too many people in the financial world have been making too much cash without earning it: That is at the root cause of this meltdown. Hedge funds, derivatives, programmed and block trading, trading or selling mortgages to other entities and then repackaging them and offering them again to a 4th or 5th party all of those maneuvers, though they have made some quick money for some, engendered and actually encouraged this crisis. The average American did not participate in this false and greedy carnival of riches, but most banks surely did! And now, of course, everyone's chief asset, one's home, has been affected. Though most Americans did little or nothing to encourage this crisis, all are paying for it. Home sales are stagnant and values have dropped precipitously. I must ask you: Is this fair?

Long before this past fall's 3 margin calls, my wife, Kate, and I knew that we would have to sell our Tupper Lake house. We knew instinctively, long before our children had any wisp of an idea, that this grand house would have to be sold. Accordingly, we have acted aggressively to make our financial position more tenable. To wit:

1) The house is listed for "x"
2) Our Vermont house has a vastly reduced sale price of "y"
3) We have borrowed "z" from relatives and friends.
4) Three boats are for sale and one has sold for already for $10,000
5) Furniture sales are actually pursued, so far netting $5,000
6) And we live frugally, buying only essentials.

More than anything, we now need your help and understanding. We believe that the margin calls, though technically legal, were unnecessary and unethical. This whole crisis, at base, was caused by improper, 3rd hand securitization: Banks should not be able to sell loans or mortgages to a 3rd party because that practice is always intrinsically destabilizing. Doctors, like yourself, are now, too late, saying the same thing; but, unless this unsafe practice is abolished, nothing will be made right.

My wife and I believe, with respect, that the Bank lost the moral high ground with last Fall's margin calls. (Let us not forget to mention the constantly changing client managers we were subjected to, the considerable losses in 2001-2002, the horrific losses in 2008, and the fact that the only superlative year was 2006). So, the question is: Do you wish to gain it, that moral high ground, back? Here is what can be done to do so:

1) Lower our 2 mortgages from 6% to 4%, with no fees or points
2) Allow a gradual pay down of the line of credit from the Trust.
3) Allow some cash flow, say "20p", from the Trust to our MRA checking account.
4) Assuming that the margin call cost us, overnight, weighty "300+", reduce the balance on our line of credit by that same amount.
5) Purchase our Tupper Lake home for "5x". It will be worth "10x" by 2015. You will make money; and it can serve as a corporate retreat in the meantime! Our current listing agreement expires 7/1/09, so the purchase could take place, without commission, the next day. It is a grand home, nearly of museum quality and one of

the showcase homes of upstate New York. Why don't you send one of your real estate people to have a look?

Doctor, these are reasonable requests from responsible and reasonable people. We have moved quickly to improve our situation. Now that the Bank has received 45 billion dollars from the government, might we not slightly benefit, as one of its long term customers? Our goal, just so you know, is to liquidate both houses as best we can, eliminating all debt and pay cash for a modest home perhaps in Delaware where I am presently applying for employment and where, importantly, property taxes are quite low, say $2000 a year for a $400,000 home. Please consider all these modest proposals.

Sincerely,

Dominic Martin

Yes, her parents are very proud of her. She has already traveled far. She has been bold and is not yet a dun which A Sea of Words tells us is "an importunate creditor or an agent employed to collect debts," (A Hexicon and Companion for Patrick O'Brians Seafaring Tales. King, Hattendork and Estes. Henry Holt, NY: 1997. P.177.) Still, I wonder if she is ever lonely in these high places? Does she have a husband to whom she might speak candidly of things at work, in some sort of late-night, wine-filled tiffin discussion or debate whereby a wider perspective might be gained, or another cause of better action found?

I muse, without proof, as a kind of monk's daydream that she is not wont of any wish to speak too closely with her male colleagues. She does not wish to curry any favors from them. She knows that she is smarter than they by jaw-dropping leagues. Surrounded by sycophants whose keenest brain is none better than hers at half effort, she does not wish to join them too often in looking through the rose-colored glass. She knows that they are lazers rather than razors, long worders who preach nothing but gauzey gauges of risk, or groat grommets, young serving men or ships' boys (<u>Brewer's</u>, p.511). In private, how else would she call them? Listless, overpaid, dons in a fancy club? 'Tis better to make a longish alphabet list. Let's! What shall she call them, fellow brewers, these arch men of green?:

1. Armchair generals,
2. friar beghards,
3. canters of mush and gruel,
4. droners,
5. euphemists,
6. swaggering fanfarons,
7. dusty gilders,
8. hanky-panky men,
9. Jacks in office,
10. kings with long hands,
11. binding lictors,
12. mandrake eaters hence sleepy,
13. nicotiners,
14. <u>odor</u> <u>lucri</u> addicts,
15. pals unmade,
16. queens of Dick,
17. wild plundering rapparees,
18. saints of Matthew, who always banks,
19. moneyed tinners who lose all battles,
20. humble pie eaters,
21. regal viscounts,
22. unlucky wanions,
23. suited yes-men or
24. drab zeroes?

What dunnage makes them think that they are so smart, these "wealthy curled darlings of our nation"? (Once again, Othello, I, 2, 69)

Still, it is clear that after all of these charges, most of them invectives, that making them, though some may be the glorious, gets me nowhere. 'Tis better to hear this: No more wear of this upon the taunted soul. Condensing them yields me no long pleasure; and thus, solely we march ahead.

Finally, she is alone and enjoys her own company more than naught.

Too, upon re-reading these 3 notes, they strike me as too feverish or stormy; if a boat she would be one, wind-tossed. In them I bounce around in an almost deranged or manic fashion. Did I not appreciate that then? In their moodiness and changeability, uncontested, today I feel embarrassed. Why had I not proof-read the 3 letters to expunge the excessive, the libelous or the repetitive? Was I too much in a pen-pusher hurry? 'Tis never a good excuse.

It is no wonder that they elicited no response. Dr. Woo never answered and does not wish to speak with us. And who can blame her? I do not. We have other, larger fish to fry. Continuing the food metaphor, as the Meyer Lanasky character says to Michael Corleone, the new godfather, in "Il Padrone", I wager that she thinks: "He's small potatoes!" Or, to quote again from my indispensable Brewer's: "To think small potatoes of it. To think very little of it, to account it of very slight worth or importance."[13] (P. 886)

So, that's us: Small potatoes! We are the smallest peoples pygmies or Lilliputians from Swifts's Gulliver's Travels. Yet, what a contrast in their attitude from 10 years ago when they fawned over us so excessively, so obsequiously, since so fervently did they seek our business. But, to quote from The Godfather once again, let us recall what Michael said to his

13 Brewer's. Cassell Publishers Ltd.: London, 1988.

mother at their estate on Lake Tahoe when he was trying to decide how best to protect the family from his weak and prodigal brother, Fredo:

"Le tempi cambiano": *The times, they change.*

Now, fellow cullies, it is time for lunch: Perhaps a gigot, and a chunk of bready fag-end. Mastications of the most fervent kind await! Tap the hogshead, Charlie, will you? Stingo anyone? 'Tis time to fight the dreaded scurvy. And now!

Notes from O'Brian's <u>Sea</u> <u>of</u> <u>Words</u>:

1. Cully: One who is cheated or imposed upon. (P. 161)
2. Gigot: A leg of lamb or veal. (P. 209)
3. Fag-end: The last part or remnant. (P. 187)
4. Hogshead: A large cask for liquid. (P.233)
5. Stingo: Strong beer or ale. (P. 405)
6. Scurvy: A disease now know to be caused by insufficient ascorbic acid (Vitamin C) in the diet. (P.379)

Bankers: Fess up: What else is not known or poorly so?

Let there be gall enough in thy ink, though thou write with a goose pen, no matter.

William Shakespeare, <u>Twelfth</u> <u>Night</u>,
III.2.47

When Fortune means to men most good, She looks upon them with a threatening eye.

William Shakespeare, <u>King</u> <u>John</u>,
III.4.119

Chapter Five:
The Bitter Barker Wars

What is a barker after all? Once again, I need to consult my friend and counselor, my always sage, the dependable <u>Brewer's</u> which defines a barker in various ways here listed:

1) Barker: A pistol which makes or barks a loud report
2) Barker: A man who stands at the entrance to a sideshow of a circus, shouting to attract customers.
3) Barking dogs seldom bite. Huffing, bounding, hectoring fellows rarely possess cool courage.
4) His bark is worse than his bite. He scolds and abuses roundly, but does not bear malice or act harshly.
5) To bark at the moon. To rail uselessly, especially at those in high places.
6) To bark up the wrong tree. To waste energy; to be on the wrong scent. (P. 82-83)

And thus it was fortuitous and resonant that, as our fortune (a word no longer apt!) dove faster and deeper than that first <u>Nautilus</u> submarine off the coast of Maine, near to the Penobscot River (the year was 1958 and I was only seven, that lucky number and Mickey's, but where was ours?), that the Bank assigned us to a Mr. Barker, here Herry Barker, Esquire, that Herry being the first, correct, and only true spelling before all later corruptions and as his parents wished, 42 years ago he was so named (may I hesitate to approximate? — at least, yes, I am allowing it so), since they were historians and liked to be exact, correct, fastidious, precise, true, accurate, and all the other cleek words impossible to miss, or hit. He, Mr. Barker, was designated by the bank to be our bone money minder, a wise captain on the pelf bridge as the sub plies northward heading for the Pole exactly fifty-two years ago today, mate.

Having never met the man, and since we do not routinely go to tea, nor slurp the darbs' buckets (a darbs being a person with money who provides entertainment, <u>Dictionary</u> <u>of</u> <u>American</u> <u>Slang</u>, p.140), I can only describe his voice or manner. Dulcet, avuncular, his oily tone bespeaks breeding and position, all the uncountable advantages of a deep and expensive schooling. His voice, resonant of a past imperialism of a culture now eclipsed by too many wars, too much spending, is one that might be selected by the BBC News — to broadcast and proclaim such earnest pluminess to the world. I ask myself?: Will it make for a later evil, or some treachery unseen? I am fearful, anxious, since all voices may hide: For example, Shakespeare writes in the <u>The</u> <u>Merchant</u> <u>of</u> <u>Venice</u>:

> "In law, what plea so tainted and corrupt
> But, being seasoned with a gracious voice,
> Obscures the show of evil"

> III. 2. 75

What will he do to us, this man who for so much power over our lives and who, task the taming voices, and gracious ones at that, hails from Britain, where, it goes without the naming, little more than a 100 years ago, he might have been a stern martinet or coddling duke, someone with beyond transcendent power. He was hired to mollify or soften our growing ire, which we commonly directed at our bungling bosuns in California who cannot find a mop, and in this capacity he was well fitted.

Just past the Ides of March, beware of all impending danger (<u>Brewer's</u>, p.583), gathering towards the start of April, 2009, I regularly felt the recurrent pull to produce a solid month's worth of letters to said Mr. Barker. I felt this urge strongly, irresistably, perhaps a little like a female animal which cannot resist estrus. (The Latin word: <u>Oestrus</u>, meaning frenzy or gadfly, pertains). I must never miss ever one day! I must never back down! Yet, I avoided the question: How does anyone vanquish an impregnable entity, like the Bank? And, why April, of all the months in the year?

Since "April is the cruelest month" (T.S. Eliot, "The Wasteland"), since Henry White describes a "peevish April day" ("Ode to Disappointment"), since April is the start of Spring when all the trees unfold their leaves, since its first day is April Fool's Day when all proper men's minds are toyed with by passion mired, mured, granted like a fox flicking at a stolen chicken, and since Shakespeare writes of "The uncertain glory of an April day" (<u>Two Gentlemen of Verona</u>, Act I, Scene 3, Line 85) — for all of those linked reasons, these tendril resonances, in April of that unglorious Spring, on a capped fool's day, and at the jester's mocking prerogative, mine, I commenced an ironic, one-way correspondence with our Mr. Barker, to entreat and to entertain, to charm and castigate, to please and to beg, and, yes, to bay and to bark, but, more than anything else, <u>as a motive to reveal dread</u>, i.e., to "Make 'em suffer," (recalling the Sudbury, Massachusetts farmer who sold his

200 acres to one George Herman Ruth, the grizzled farmer exhorting that meanest order to the Babe, to beat the New York Yankees — (Thank you, Mr. John Fusco, who wrote the 1992 screenplay for <u>The</u> <u>Babe</u> in which he describes that Boston Red Sox fan.)

> he, too, hearing in his
> brain the plaintive refrain
> "Before The Trade..."
> "Before The Trade..."

thinking, like a fool or twit, that if I might engender even the smallest dust of shame, or elicit the tiniest suggestion of apology, that some trifle measure by the navy blue suit wearers might emerge, something which might, in turn, help our family. It is the slimmest of preposterous hopes, but this one I'll defend. I wonder: Does he think me some dumb paddy Irish? Yes. He knows that I am not Mossbauser, nor Moseley. The British have often thought less of those of us from the smaller island. Down the nose. Down the years.

So, may we consider them as notes between competing generals in a war, one which is full of strife and alarm, as meanest words and overstated cases, attempts at a caustic humor which fall absolutely flat, and lines only meant to mock and defame? Always, Murf, they would have been sent quite early in the morning so that HB would see them the first thing, to stake out the day's saucy and combative tone, to worsen the alarm and make more full all mistrust. By look or crook! Mustered onwards! One grabs, as one can, a thistle, the Scottish sign of defiance.

* * *

The men, on the other hand, one can tell, I do not feel so kindly towards... HA!

47

* * *

Thus commences <u>argumentum</u> <u>ad</u> <u>crumenam</u>, an argument relating to the purse, ours, which once was and now is mostly lost; but, what's the bother?

"Ruin has taught me thus to ruminate" (William Shakespeare, Sonnet 64; Line 11), and why not?

Dear Mr. Barker,

Would you please converse with our attorney, XX of XX regarding whether our two mortgages qualify under the federal program (40% do, per our president) for principal and interest rate reductions, and if not, why not? I suggest that if the latter is the case it is because the loans were sold to a 3rd entity, a practice which must be curtailed. We need your help now. There have been two months of talk. We have put both our homes for sale, have cars and boats for sale, are renting out the main house as of June 1, are renting out our Vermont house May 25, are dickering for employment in Virginia at $60,000 a year; but, as you know, everything is selling for 50-60 cents on the dollar, resulting in a continued erosion of wealth. Clearly, we have done and will continue to do all that is possible to "right the ship." Who killed the housing market: The mouse in my pocket or your cousin, Larry? It is now your turn.

Sincerely,

D. M.

Dear Mr. Barker,   4/2/2009

In 2002, when I noted a large purchase of Oracle, at a price which had, by then, already precipitously fallen, I was told to be quiet and not to question the experts, that Oracle's price would return to where it should be, that the purchase had not been made just before the tech bubble burst.

False assumptions all.

D. M.

Dear Mr. Barker, 4/3/2009

It used to be, 35 years ago, that bankers were among the most cautious and prudent among us, disinclined to gamble or be, in any way, reckless with the funds with which they had been so carefully entrusted.

What happened to alter this dynamic? Or does anyone really care?

D. M.

Dear Mr. Barker,   4/4/2009

For at least 2 decades, bankers' normal caution and prudence have morphed to a gambling recklessness. Was this due to the surfeit of people in the business, all trying to justify extravagant pay and bonuses? Ten percent of Harvard graduates used to work in the financial field; yet, today, that number is 40%.

D. M.

Dear Mr. Barker,   4/5/2009

With all those bright brains flocking to the industry, it is no wonder that a competitive free-for-all broke out: Who could come up with the most clever, most profitable, yet most unpredictable financial entitities where, without strenuous effort, the Bank could make easy profits? That person would rise in stature and rank, no matter how foolhardy were his proposals. A frenzy of churning and skimming!

D. M.

Dear Mr. Barker,   4/6/2009

For political reasons, both parties under the uncertain and untrained eye of Mr. Barney Frank of Massachusetts sought to increase the percentage of people owning, rather than renting, homes. Accordingly, Fannie Mae and Freddie Mac lowered significantly the terms under which potential homeowners might qualify for loans. May of these loans were "back-end loaded" with much higher interest rates after an initial lower-rate year or two. In this greedy rush, no one, it seems, bothered to foretell the high rate of foreclosures and the resulting "freeze-up" of the housing market.

D. M.

Dear Mr. Barker,   4/7/2009

Hedge funds, which had scarcely existed before, were dreamt up by financial advisors trying to find an easy way to make a considerable return with little real or productive effort: Sooners. Aided by a complacent Congress, who thought <u>not</u> to regulate them, these entitities sprang into existence, suddenly, by the 100s, and then, by the 1000s. Many of their managers made easy millions, if not, billions. Now, many have collapsed, harming millions of families across our country. Why was Congress so asleep? Because its members took the money.

                                                    D. M.

Dear Mr. Barker,   4/8/2009

Derivatives: Who among us can explain them who cannot also delineate differential equations, linear algebra or numerical analysis? Must we rely on Kalman's filters and smoothers to make a reasonable rate of return? Such was the greedy stampede to engender new, arcane, and impossible-to-understand mechanisms that we, this nation, allowed the derivatives to be backed by the aforementioned, toxic mortgages from Fannie Mae and Freddie Mac. Thank you, Mr. Frank and Mr. and Mrs. Gramm. They showed much chutzpah to act surprised when this house of cards collapsed. Should it not have been predicted? By whom?

                                                    D. M.

Dear Mr. Barker, 4/9/2009

In the old days before "churning," banks would retain their loans, i.e., they would <u>not</u> package or sell them to a 3rd party. A banker would no more sell those loans than he would loan out his tractor or wife (regardless of order). That way, they would stay in close contact with the mortgage holder, to warm and protect him, as well as the banker's money. Now, since we have become so "sophisticated", that practice is seen as terribly old-fashioned; yet, until we return to it, this problem of improper securitization will doom all other, or further attempts at reform.

D. M.

Dear Mr. Barker,   4/10/2009

The other day there was an interesting bit on National Public Radio which you might have enjoyed. It described a non-Amish banker in Pennsylvania who catered only to the Amish there. He knows them very well, their close and extended families, their various businesses, their medical histories — you name it. Pointedly, he retains all his loans to them; he does not package them up or sell them off. And, guess what, he has no bad loans! And, accordingly, his bank is not in trouble! Don!: What a novel idea! Take a memo, Myrtle!

D. M.

Dear Mr. Barker,   4/11/2009

One other thing must be mentioned so that a full picture
of this heedless melange of speculation, untested entitities
and unknown theories may be sketched out: The repeal, two
years ago, of the "uptick rule." This unfortunate action made
short selling easier, pleasing the churner and day-traders and
hurting the chances for success, i.e., a reasonable rate of
return, for the average American investor who lives in Des
Moines. Why did not someone in the SEC say, "Hold on!"?
The main characters have already been corrupted.

                                              D. M.

Dear Mr. Barker,   4/12/2009

When we first invested substantially with the Bank ten
years ago, we were incessantly told that the smartest way
to invest was the "Buy and Hold." So, we did and look
what happened! For, is there not an inherent contradiction
between that philosophy of caution, and the reckless and destabilizing financial instruments that I have described one
by one. Despite the headlong rush towards these dangerous
strategies, was there not someone who understood that they
were, and are, contrary to the Bank's long-standing view: To
buy stocks and to hold them is the best way to make money.
A division exists within your own house.

                                              D. M.

Dear Mr. Barker,   4/13/2009

Perhaps if all these dangerous instruments and strategies had not been introduced to the market at essentially the same time, the outcome may have been different. If they had been put in place more gradually, intrinsic flaws might have been more easily detected and corrected. This is, then, fundamentally an issue of <u>PACE</u>. To implement them, all these untested mechanisms, <u>simultaneously</u> was clear folly and symptomatic of an underlying greed. Instead, indeed, the rules of Warren Stephens of Stephens Incorporated ought to have been followed: "Build Things Slowly."

D. M.

Dear Mr. Barker,   4/14/2009

Thus, for at least two decades caution has changed to gambling, prudence has morphed to recklessness. In the midst of this dangerous melange we have all lost sight of two ideas:

1) There are too many people in the business, and
2) What the bankers have been doing is not fundamentally productive.

Yet, most bankers will not suffer. Look at Goldman-Sachs' very decent first quarter announced yesterday. Indeed, the high pay, unearned fees and Christmas bonuses roll on, unabated.

D. M.

Dear Mr. Barker,   4/15/2009

When I was in the wine business (to which I may be returning), we were heavily and carefully regulated by the Treasury Department. The BATF told us what to do, what forms to file, etc.

On the other hand, the financial industry has been unfettered. Does a degree of collusion exist? Why are federal anti-trust statutes routinely unenforced? Why did the SEC ignore, for many years, complaints about Bernie Madoff?

This lack of real regulation has allowed a financial oligarchy, a government by the few, to form. It must be dismantled if we are to get our country back.

D. M.

Dear Mr. Barker,   4/16/2009

For years, too much closeness has existed between financial institutions and the government. Fannie Mae and Freddie Mac have been called "quasi-government": Was that not asking for a heap of trouble, now received? Why was the Bank's recent purchase of _____, clearly in violation of anti-trust laws, both federal and state, allowed to stand? Answer: Collusion, or the king and the police are too close. Then, a Bank becomes "too big to fail". Who allowed it to become too big? And who suffers?: The little guy, per usual.

D. M.

Dear Mr. Barker,   4/17/2009

Some say more regulation is the answer: As long as we
have keen-eyed and eager regulators at every turn, all will
be well. Yet, as we have seen with Chris Cox of the SEC,
who watched while Madoff waltzed, many regulators have
ties <u>too</u> <u>close</u> to Wall Street to be effective. The financial
world and the people meant to corral them are friends: How
can they be dispassionate and zealous? Besides, and more
importantly, the whiz-bang Young Turks will find a way
around the regulations anyway, using that old phrase: Find
the loophole and fill it!

D. M.

Dear Mr. Barker,   4/18/2009

Did not any think-tank person at the Bank read the book:
<u>Too</u> <u>Big</u> <u>to</u> <u>Fail</u> by two Minnesota financial analysts,
Feldman and Stearn? Many years ago they made the same
argument that I am making now: That many banks have
gotten too big, that those are the <u>only</u> <u>ones</u> with big balance-
sheet problems, and if the feds had enforced the anti-trust
laws, which were put in place after the Depression to
prevent things like the '08 collapse from happening, this
debacle would have been avoided. The relationship between
government and the financial industry is <u>too</u> <u>close</u>.

D. M.

Dear Mr. Barker,   4/19/2009

We hired the bank to earn a return at 7%, 2% over bonds, yet you did not do it. If the personnel at the bank had been as adept at making money (their job!) as they had been at making margin calls, those margin calls would not have been necessary. Ours is a fiduciary relationship: Therefore, if the bank wishes to save itself, it must help all those people it has harmed.

D. M.

Dominic M. Martin

Dear Mr. Barker,   4/20/2009

Our plan had been, before this avoidable debacle ensued, to sell our 6-acre Vermont home. At the time we put it on the market exactly 2 years ago, we listed it for 3X. We intended to use the considerable equity to pay down our line of credit by that amount. Instead, nothing has happened except that we have reduced the price by 1X. What is essentially a crisis of <u>finances</u> has carried over to <u>real</u> <u>estate</u>. Eventually, home prices will return to what was normal (excess speculation only occurred in 4 states), but in the meantime we, as well as millions of other distressed Americans, may have to sell it at a low price, once again "confirming losses."

D. M.

Dear Mr. Barker,   4/21/2009

Ten years ago we met our builder. For some years, all went
well: He gave close estimates, watched his crew, yelled at
them when necessary, and built mistake-free structures.
Soon, though, he lost the plot. Gradually, his estimates
loosened, his crew smoked marijuana, mistakes appeared
like pimples and punch-lists were commonly ignored. In
February 2007, I asked him how much it would take to
finish our main house (now for sale). He said "x". It turned
out to be more like 4x, hence, our current crisis. But, why is
this important to you? Answer: Bankers should care about
the bank <u>and</u> their customers.

D. M.

Dear Mr. Barker,   4/22/2009

So, we have seen the unhappy simultaneity of 3 factors:

1) a failure to sell our Vermont home
2) a greedy builder whom we foolishly trusted
3) a stock market which lost 41% of its value in 2008.

Unacceptable. The Banks' inability to make money for its customers represents a high failure of performance. Do you now accept <u>any</u> responsibility?

Ours was, and is, a fiduciary relationship wherein we trusted you, based on your glowing reputation, consistent statements, and immodest proposals, to make money. To repair that relationship we need your help now.

D. M.

Dear Mr. Barker,   4/23/2009

Hell! We not only need your help but, the Bank <u>owes</u> <u>us</u>
— after all the false promises, the bungling of my IRA, the
disastrous results of our 3 children's IRAs, the inability to
predict the tech bubble's busting, the constantly revolving
door of managers (two of whom I never even met, one
because he was not paying attention to the site of the
meeting), the unethical margin calls which only confirmed
losses, as I mentioned yesterday, to the tune of at least "5X"
— all of this after the bank promised us strict attention to
detail and that unheard of word: PROFIT!

D. M.

Dear Mr. Barker,   4/24/2009

Acting quickly and pro-actively in the past 5 months, we have sold one wooden boat and one tractor. Virtually everything else we own is for sale, but, given the economic collapse we are now witnessing, something engendered by corporate greed and a yawning government's inattention, most people do not have any money. Therefore, it is very difficult to sell anything, and if something does sell, it sells at 50 cents on the dollar, once again, confirming losses. We also cashed in our Edward Jones account and my IRA, both, once again, at <u>huge</u> losses. Thanks for nothing!

D. M.

Dear Mr. Barker,   4/25/2009

We have offered up for sale a 1939 Chris Craft Sportsman Utility, a stunningly restored version for which we paid approximately ____. We have received, after 4 months, <u>no</u> offers. Once again we will be lucky to receive 50 cents on the dollar.

Also, we have offered up for sale a 1955 Jaguar XK140 Drop Head Coupe for which we also paid approximately _____. It, perhaps, will sell somewhat more easily, but that remains to be seen. Everything is selling slowly, if at all, and at poor prices. You can see our active commitment to right the ship. But, <u>where</u> <u>is</u> <u>your</u> <u>aid?</u>

                                              D. M.

Dear Mr. Barker,   4/26/2009

Because of our difficult economic situation, we have put our Tupper Lake home, which took 8 years and _____ many many dollars to build, up for sale. Also, I have applied at 50 schools and 20 wineries. However, due to the economic crisis, engendered by gambling greed in the financial world and governmental lassitude, jobs are very hard to find, and the economy continues to constrict. Ten percent unemployment exists. Next month, we will move our family from the "big house" to the guest house to generate some rental income. What more would you have us do? Happy?

D. M.

Dear Mr. Barker,   4/27/2009

You should know that, absent a miracle of some sort, we do not have the funds in our checking account to cover the May 3 and May 5 mortgage deductions. Accordingly, we need and <u>are</u> <u>due</u> your immediate attention. Please do 2 things:

1) Cut the 2 payments in half
2) Move _____ from the trust to the MRA. We have not touched it in 6 months. Since most of it is bonds (if my orders were followed!), it has earned _____. That amount will tide us over until rental income here becomes substantial in July.

                                                    D. M.

Dear Mr. Herry Barker,   4/28/2009

Fiduciary: Of, having to do with, or involving a confidence or trust.

Collusion: A secret agreement for a fraudulent purpose. Study Paulson's pressure on Lewis to absorb Merrill Lynch quietly.

Many of your folks live in a bubble.

In a week we will not be able to buy milk or write checks.

D. M.

Dear Mr. Barker,   4/29/2009

Did the Martin family engineer this financial collapse? Did
our 8 year old daughter design hedge funds or derivatives?
Were we in charge of A.I.G.?

The Bank has cost us a fortune. Is the plan to foreclose,
costing us another fortune? We never should have allowed
the Bank to sell off any loans since that action creates the
triangle which is something my father warned me about.
People should not be able to say, "It cannot be helped!" We
need time, NOW, to sell the house which, we realize, we
cannot afford.

The ripples continue: The other week I lost a well-paying
job because the school at which I worked as an adjunct
closed the full time job search. The president of the school
said that the change of direction was because of the poor
economy, which as we know, was engendered by a compliant
government, and a reckless financial industry.

D. M.

Dear Mr. Barker,   4/30/2009

For this, my last note of April, the cruellest month, I will say
the truest thing: Banks should not earn fees automatically.
When a client's trust tanks, as ours did in 2008, it is unethical
for any bank to collect fees. This explains how financial
industry profits as a percentage of US business profits went
from 8% in 1950 to 27% in 2007. Fee taking made our
trust tank more! They should be calculated quarterly on
a graduated, incentive-based manner, like the rest of the
business world. Unless this kind of populism returns, banks
will remain a place only for the big-shots.

D. M.

* * *

So I reread again, for the near hundredth time these nasty letters, an act quite separate in time and manner from their composition; and, yes, some do seem, at first blush, mean, as in mean-spirited. I task myself: In arguing a case, can one go too far, or over the edge? I think of the bridge at Remagen: Too far? Is it better to press less resolutely, especially when one is trying to garner a concession? I think of that acerbic line from George Patton's journals:

"There is no use getting into a pissing match with a skunk."[14]

But then again, my mind revolves further and settles on the firmest ground thinking: Bankers have become isolated, set apart, another nation, one which can make up, pretty much, its own rules. They can do no wrong, since, when they make mistakes, the government, i.e., their former colleagues, bails them out! Friends and acquaintances regulate them, or are supposed to do so. Impossible! They, <u>sotto voce</u>, pass the word to government regarding what they want, their druthers, and, as I used to say as a kid, "Presto Magico!", it happens. Such power they have! But, how shady!

Of course, it happens that members of this moneyed fraternity (for it is largely men) tend to socialize together, take vacations together, and join the same golf club. Typically, because of their Christmas bonuses, their annual wages might triple or more, much more. After awhile, after, say, 5 years of receiving their exorbitant bonuses and salaries, it is normal that they would begin to feel greatly entitled to them. They expect them, as happens. With time's passage, a process of corrosion or slippage, they would perceive these most immodest paychecks as their due, and not as old rope

---

14   Quoted from <u>General Patton: A Soldier's Life</u>, by Stanley P. Hirshson; Harper Collins, NY 2002, p. 585-6.

since "money for old rope is easy money," (<u>Brewer's,</u> p. 963). Especially with the quarter's passage of time and surrounded by scores of other bankers similarly overly paid, they would make the case that every penny, every ducat, every farthing has been earned. Every one! A miracle!

These lucky ones, our new nobles, have been cast (as if in a play or dream) to join an exclusive and extravagant club, one which, because of government's dundering and always growing lassitude and the financial institutions' burgeoning power, can more or less make its own rules. They skate around the corners. They can tell the government that they do not wish tighter rules to govern hedge funds, for example, and the government, compliant or inattentive or both, says, simply, "Fine." That is one of near countless examples I might make, so embedded is the collusion within the oligarchy.

Bankers' condescension and arrogance towards their customers, no, all citizens, serves to confirm that they live in a large and calculated bubble. Sadly, the government, instead of pricking that bubble, coddles it, protecting it, making it grow stronger day by day. Every month, neigh, every week, financial institutions grow every stronger. Their plungers are tipsters becoming more insulted and more protected, farming a tyranny unseen. Banks remind me of octopuses whose tentacles go everywhere and squeeze voraciously whatever it is that they hold.

Where is the attitude of excellence, nastiness and meanness meant to control this growing behemoth? How ought it to be engendered? Who will do this necessary job? Or, is it this: Forget it, Jake; we are no longer a nation united, <u>e</u> <u>pluribus</u> <u>unum</u>, but an oligarchy controlled by renards, foxes, those few anointed ones steeped in privilege and access, those who can do no wrong and who happily practice the unkind dictum:

> Heads I win;
> Tales you lose.

Here lies the difficulty (hare): <u>Hic</u> <u>jacet</u> <u>lepus</u>. In fewer words: Is the big battle over, or the war already done?

So, all of this means that I do not apologize one whit for the uncivil tone of these many missives to Mr. Barker. Indeed, untypically, perhaps I have <u>undercharged</u> him and the profligate Bank. Thus, they are too weak, too timid. Upon rereading these letter I think that they are not caustic enough. I have committed the little know sin of using "Too Much Charity". Ha! In this small uprising, the time for civility is over.

Since, have they not harmed, nearly, the entire country and all of her citizens? Have not the self-interested banks, with the meltdown of 2008, committed upon our nation a self-made, huge treachery, that crime which will not say its name? Therefore, rather than further coddled and protested, should they not be spoken to sternly, as one does to an errant child out back by the woodshed in clearest tones not caressing?

When one asks most of them a simple question: Who is responsible for Wall Street losing 40% of its value in 2008?, they never blame themselves. They never think to blame themselves. Instead, they will say that these things can happen, washing their hands of any responsibility just like Pontius Pilate did. If they see not the error of their ways, how does one make them so see? Or, am I going too fast now, like Jehu, "that coachman who drives at a rattling pace?"[15]

For, what bankrobbers will attest to the crime? It is not human nature that the shameless man will not admit to

---

15 <u>Brewer's</u>. p.608

shame? Cannot a carouser be trained to deny all fault? Most will deny all wrongdoing and, but, deny yet again.

Further, what adulterer says, "Yes. I have been unfaithful." What student confesses to cheating on an exam unless he fears apprehension, opprobrium, and punishment? So large and insular is this bubble that encloses the world of banks that these bollixed-up boys have lost most of their moral compasses. Christian business ethics? Gone, like dust. Since the government, charged with regulation but not doing it, is weak, the banks can make their own rules and think their own thoughts. They may think, for example, with Nietzsche and all the egoists, kam kam or crooked kings, that "If I am happy, the world is happy."

Yet, in this land of Lethe or forgetfulness (Brewer's, p. 661), the bankers have ignored the oldest of business propositions: All business ought to be a two-way street. That is to say, I must respect my customer. I must protect my customer. If they are unhappy, I have a problem. If I do not treat him well, I may lose him. Clearly, in this only the most recent collapse, bankers thought too little of their clients, and far too much of themselves.

This two-way street idea needs further explication. I used to be in the wine business as a winemaker. Obviously, then, my own palette was crucial in how I assembled blends: A wine had to be most pleasing to me before I could accept it.

However, my palette was slightly skewed: I tended to like wine with slightly more acid than most. They were, to me, more refreshing and more compatible with foods.

So, a quandary arose: Do I make wines for myself, or for others, that is, the average consumer? Obviously, I had to think about what the typical wine drinker might prefer, and neglect my own choices since, no matter how hard I might struggle I could not drink all the wine!

Thus, a two-way street emerged in the winery. I became used to and had to think about what the client or the customer preferred. And that is how and why I am so disturbed and so angry with the Bank and its rank and haughty employees, all these who routinely renounced our opinions: They clearly cared little for their clients, us; and they were concerned, disproportionately, for themselves. This constitutes a new tyranny and is bad business.

May I say any of this or should I be silent? May one demur amongst our new nobles? Sometimes, no, often, the First Amendment?: Is it used up, exhausted? May I speak? Can I protest any of the razzle-dazzle? Can anyone? Who decides, who may speak? Don't I risk derision in castigating these powerful forces? Who dares to speak against them? Knowing that the colluding king and police will gauge my words as unapt, should I say nothing? But, why should we take their word as true, those ones whose ox is never gored?

This reminds me of a scene in the movie "Express." Syracuse Coach Schwartzwalder is protesting the brutal treatment that his black halfback, Ernie Davis, is getting; the refs are complicit, wanting him hurt and to leave the game. One says to the angry coach, "That's one. You've been warned." The coach fires back, "What are you: My first grade teacher?" Can't American's raise hell anymore? Is Mr. Barker my daddy gone bad?

Perhaps I might guess the reader's thought: That I become a fool in scolding and defaming so resolutely, and too, if I wish to gain any small advantage I would be wise to praise his lordship without a waiver.

But I say: No, since once an Irishman has his dander up, that temper will not easily cool. I have become Myles Crawford who says, in James Joyce's <u>Ulysses</u>, that an opponent:

"..can Kiss My Royal Irish Arse. Myles Crawford
cried (that) loudly over his shoulder. Any time he
likes, tell him."

KMRIA. It is good to be the downtrodden, the better to
fight. Let's get in a rhubarb; why not! A donnybrook or
commotion! Yes! Are you saying I'd be better off sending
to him some damn mash note? No! Anyone who defends
the Big Club is a gimp artist and con man. Gestate! Why
should I not at least try to put the chill on him so that
he feels a little out of sorts. I'm just the rock in his show,
someone he unpleasantly thinks about before nodding off.
He will admit to no unjustice, none, since he has been
trained (re: brainwashed) by the Really Big Guys to never
apologize. I know this rich nob looks down his long nose
on me as if I were one more Paddy rustic or groundling at
the show, riff-raff cattle, someone unschooled, unlearned,
unknowledgeable and all the other un's. We Irish are used
to being called dull swine, Mick bastards, potato heads,
narrowbacks, boghoppers, oat eaters, sozzled Quinns,
Shamrocks, you name it but can't tame it: Then, too, there's
our speedy willingness to bring rancor fast and hard to any
sort of ruckus or double-cross fight.

And, why is that? Three hundred years of English
contempt, maltreatment, and neglect visited upon the Irish,
the tenant farming and carnages and all the other inhumane
privations, must have put a genetic stamp on my psyche, one
telling me that if someone wishes unfairness toward me, to
condescend or go for an upset angle, that in quick response
I will be ready to roar, to thunder, to crusty bellow, to at
least try to leave some mark on the cheek or mind. To defy
any tyranny is the first step of a free man.

After all, we are dealing with a group that has never
mentioned <u>one word</u> of apology to our family, <u>one sentence</u>

devoted to the moral responsibility they share with us, or <u>one</u> <u>paragraph</u> of conciliation on any subject. It staggers me now to think again about how insulated these gents must be, how separate their lives are from average Americans who do not receive colossal bonuses at Christmas. It overwhelms me to consider how thick must be the bubble that coddles and cocoons them, making all those outside it low commoners and all those fortunate enough to be inside friends of kings. Finally, an obvious further thought arises: Is this the best our nation can do? Is the establishment of collusion at the oligarchy wise? Is this pestilent condition what the Founding Fathers envisioned? Are these extravagant salaries and bonuses, whether paid for out of taxpayers' monies or not, a benefit to all our peoples, or do they not drive an ever-growing wedge among the classes? About all of this, and more, we must think again.

To avert, all of these questions of cole (an old country term for money (<u>Brewer's</u>, p. 256), once more, I shall address in the coda: How to fix this Gold-Brick Mess at this small work's conclusion; and, until then, let us speak of other, more various things: Pranks and jests or what you will; to tingle and tantalize, to bring a humored smile to a dullard's face, mine, to erase a wrinkle even if crudely done, for to live too sad a life, is to only look backward. It allays no fear, but only grows it. Shakespeare advises that one ought to be like Yorik "a fellow of finite jest." (<u>Hamlet</u>, V.1.184). Methinks he's right. Therefore, let us sail now to the lubber's hole, boon companions all, let us dally now to the lubber's hole,[16] and let us do so quickly, quickly, since our ship, she is in the keenest trouble.

---

16 <u>Brewer's</u>: Lubber's hole: Some way of evading or wriggling through one's difficulties. p.688

Under the placid surface, at least the way I see it, there are really disturbing trends: huge imbalances, disequilibria, risks - call them what you will. Altogether the circumstances seem to me to be as dangerous and intractable as any I can remember, and I can remember quite a bit.

> - Paul Volcker in a speech at Stanford in February 2005, Quoted in House of Cards. P. 293

That's the Irish people all over - they treat a joke as a serious thing and a serious thing as a joke.

> Sean O'Casey (1880-1964) from The Shadow of a Gunman. (1923)

When angry, count four; when very angry, swear.

> Mark Twain (1835-1910) from Pudd'nhead Wilson. 1894

He knows nothing; and he thinks he knows everything: That points clearly to a political career.

> George Bernard Shaw (1856-1950) from Major Barbara. 1907

The strain is rather tough and I'll be glad when this mess is over."

> Said by Major General Terry de la Mesa Allen on April 22, 1943 right before the American Army's 1st Armored Division pushed into Tunis; Quoted by Rick Atkinson's Book: An Army at Dawn: The War in North Africa, 1942-1943 Henry Holt and Co.: New York, NY. P. 500.

The nervous system's individual imprint means that some are better than others at handling the pressure.

William Bradley Martin, MD
circa 1997

Chapter Six:
Diatribes. Diagnostics. Diaspora.

Chance, there might have been another "D": Disparate as in "Completely distinct or different in kind; entirely dissimilar." A "split mind," one schizophrenic, intruded, stoked by monstrous financial pressures and anxiety's constant uncertainty. Though we were not alone in this dismemberment or scattering of limbs, <u>disjecta</u> <u>membra</u>, that cold thought granted no succor: How to feed the kids? How? Is all crashing down? Pretty much. This looming lurking monster of debt stalks every corner, kills every moment that might be briefly joyous, and presages a future beyond dismal if I let it so. No. Thus, that incessant gloom must be dismissed out of hand since it does no good, and gathers to it little courage.

One thinks and conjures, ruminates and dreams upon strange dreams which spin and turn the more.

Over time, the strain of no money makes for still stranger thoughts. "Now is the winter of our discontent made glorious summer by this sun of York." (William Shakespeare, <u>Richard</u> <u>III</u>; I.1.1.) Strangest, mocking, doubled dreams then intrude, recede, return again. Nights are not spent slept well. Gossamer threads of dark color and envelop these midnight conjurings, half thoughts all, and most lead me astray disquieted, or slip to obscure cul-de-sacs the most blind.

Once, I passed a better night, dreaming past the Irati and Isonzo, that I had been a soldier entering a conquered city, mine, whose peoples cheer me manfully as I stride on. I have just been crowned by an olive's garland placed by boys. As I walk on, because of the noise, I scarcely hear the small notice in my ear that says, "All glory is fleeting." I reflect on Shakespeare's line:

> "Vain promp and glory of this world, I hate ye: I feel my new heart opened. O! How wretched is that poor man that hangs on princes' favours!" (<u>King Henry VIII</u>, III.2.366.)

I wonder: Is there a change afoot, some new measure of grace??

Yes, a tale repeated, but are not all tales at least twice or thrice told? There is nothing new under the sun, again: Ecclesiastes I, 2. Yet, I wish to make a diaspora or fast diaspersion whereby this awful dream or nightmare of pelf might go away; but, most nights were not so pleasantly passed.

To exorcize these demons cruel, I began, as one does, to write and scribble, to form cleaver, cleaver thoughts the better to attach, and to make the devil go away, to chase him gone down the rutted lane. They are notes and asides, these letters and treatises, all sorts of mean mutterings. Some remnants are dreamt only, verses left as diffuse and wandered scratches on a notepad next to our bed. Some tagends are diffuse snippets of crazed doggerel which, when shorn of context, lose all meaning when looked at later.

Still, they show a certain flavor of mind, one held still in the midst of a mindless fray. They may be educative or amusing, what you will. Hence, this book: to expunge, to expiate, to exorcise all evil spirits and, thus, to live again. And I think: This storm has hit the whole nation.

NOTES:

I think of this short word: Fiasco. The word was used by the glassblowers of Venezia, the old city, (on Murano? Burano? Torcello? La quale isola?) to describe bad workmanship and it may have some allusion to the bursting of a bottle. Sounds true. Italian: a flask (Brewer's p. 423) "utter failure, ridiculous breakdown." Sounds familiar? Its use today is most apt, or may I say so, dishers? Spongers? Those that always stay alert?

* * *

As time goes by, I think of all the other cousins who are hard hit; and that this avoidable mess is a natural disaster ignored by most sources of news. Too, I recall a boxer staggering about the ring, someone first named Giacobbe, his mind spinning, raging, crazily; he can think in staccato bursts only, milione scatterings, rent and renegade glimpses that have neither start nor tail. If studied long enough, they make a portrait of a foggy, early morning crash, of a boat or plane or car, making the physics all extending, unstoppingly in mid-sentence. All parts fly. They may be written by Retiarius, the gladiator who always used a net thrown over his adversaries to subdue them. (Brewer's, p. 944) But, before the battle can be joined, one must recognize the enemy. That is: To see his face.

* * *

1. Easter Sunday: Such unnecessary consternation: Ethics? Out the window, nowadays. Gone, like dust behind a Masterati Polvere.

2. Corporations are today greater than the government. Wall Street is now bigger than the land of Lincoln. How did this happen? Voles or moles? Asleep, we were.

3. Trust was given since all people cannot know all. Fiduciary.
   Erasmus (1466? - 1536): The last man who did.

4. The children's 529 funds: The grifters will say they will return to prior levels. Horsedung. We no longer trust their inferior Lenin speeches about the future. Kibitzers who do not finish what they start.

5. Gladly we shall soon subsist, only. Then, these tendril lucubrations will cease, and we must then look for jokes anywhere that they may be found.

6. You will lose this argument because you are on the wrong side. Peccant, guilty, sinful: Can anyone around here say the word, or has it too gone away?

7. Certainly, the Bank acted as a catalytic agent for a precipitative reaction that would have happened, more slowly, anyway. A chemistry experiment gone terribly awry.

8. Do you folks know what you have done to this once-great country? The old folks who are financially cleaned out. Who cares? You? Who speaks for the little old lady who is now busted?

9. You people think that you can pull this egregious, large stunt and get away with it; and in the sleepy eyes of the Associated Press, you just may: complicity.

10. In basketball, being pushed around under the basket, one soon learns how to push back. With force and the elbows up, akimbo, bent like a bow, but upward.

11. You ought to pay for these thoughts since they will vastly improve your business. Here's my bill.

12. Reynard's Globe of Glass: Great promises, no scores, vulpine and clever foxes, that great French word: Renards.

13. I do not know what more you clowns could do to our family and many others.

14. Did I invent the idea of mortgage backed securities, soon to become toxic , or was it the beyond clever mouse in my pocket that laid that nasty turd?

15. What non-miracles you perform for strangers. Unearned fees make all my replies churlish. Inutile. Useless comments unless we re-invent ourselves completely.

16. The shameless man — How can he be shamed, or is that by definition impossible?

17. Why do we all accept the advice of experts, those so-called. Recall the Bay of Pigs. Kennedy in April, 1962 at Bahia de Puercos.

18. These folks have no idea of the depth of seething anger across this country. These guys can be this unaware because of the bubble. These fellows only talk to each other. Group think at the

golf club. Who is paying for the next round of drinks?

19. Interrupting Guerra continually, I did not wish to hear her complaints, her motivations, her justifications, or her muddied rationales. Always employing the triangle when she cannot get something done.

20. The lance-corporal, experienced in battle, is always closing the drapes against the opaque, dunnish slay. He does not wish to see. Occlusion. Suddenly, tenders, there is a flash of lightning, an éclaircissement across the slay. Just as quickly, it subsides. He says to himself: "Nothing is in sight which is not grey."

21. The Retort Corteous: "Sir, I am not of your opinion. I beg to differ from you. May I? It joins the Quip Modest, Reply Churlish, Reproof Valiant, Countercheck Quarrelsome. May I speak, sir, elf, dwarf, or is my capacity gone away down the rabbits' hole, too? (Brewer's, p. 944)

22. All the smarty-pants, (Big Time Operators: BTO) said to invest in stocks and real estate. We did exactly that, and look what happened. Disaster. Calamity. Futile.

23. Most of what the cakes (Obsolete slang for a half-baked fool. Brewer's, p.182) knew was contravened, rescended, or erased - yet, little frank discussion of that has taken place. Who goes backwards anymore to analyse?

24. This story reminds me of the West Texas farmhand who drinks beer while driving his truck down the dusty road, always throwing his spent cans away from the front of the vehicle.

Clever fellow. He drives a Dodge because he likes the name.

25. Did my eight year old daughter come up with credit default swaps or "risk-free" arbitrage, and I just missed it?

26. I thought that we hired you rascals, you tricksters, you knaves, to make money, not to lose it. It's time to raise Cain, chappie. Let's begin.

27. We were ignored and made fun of. They always conveyed the impression that their brain power was superior, and that they alone were privy to a vast wealth of knowledge which nobody else would study or could ever know. Still.

28. Today's financial people do not make or create wealth. Instead, they churn and skim whey. Spent grains. The dregs. What in the wine business we all less.

29. The idea of assigning fees when stocks have only lost money is counter to all proper business instincts. They should only be collected <u>after</u> profit has been earned, quarterly, and on a graduated basis. Not a radical idea, but it will be labeled as such by the "boys in the know", who are now happy as a clam at high tide; they are full of chinck, awash in moolah. (<u>Brewer's</u>, p.229) Money: so called because it chinks or jingles in the purse. Or used to.

   However, here's a little recess, to get more fresh air in the lungs. Why not? Let us speak about all the words for money: Stamps, clacker, bawbee, oscar, do-re-mi, the needful, lettuce, juice, coin, boo-boo, scrip, plunk, pile, oof, and mon -

Not, that's not right since there are tads and scallions more, Ted: Mr. Young Onion: Grease, pudding, tab, libra, wagon wheel, yen; and unless you know them all and will never forget one, then maybe you'd be smart to be a little more cautious: Got it, Zelda? A female square. And don't forget: Quiff, salve, folding or happy cabbage, cucumber, flush, buffo, wafers, pelf, D, sinker, not hay, scratch, sow, buck, double sawbuck, soap, jingle-jangle, clams, bread — I'd say this if I were not interrupted:

Maybe someone ought to give these limping, derelict schmoes a pop quiz asking for the clear definition to each one, and, if they get <u>even</u> <u>one</u> befuddled or wrong, they can no longer eat the strudel, but have to get a real job. A small voice whispers to my Irish pee brain: Ah, don't be such a gloomy crape-hanger. Still, think of all they need to know, and didn't. They did not know how much they did not know. That's it, Margaret! The whole enchilada or dogwood, taquito or hers, pollo mole or hoagie! Hells-bells, they thought they could predict the future, tell us what would happen tomorrow. If that is not arrogance, I don't know what is! (Number 29 is the longest since 1929 was the longest year? But, one takes one's lumps).

30. As John F. Kennedy says 3/4 of the way through "Thirteen Days", the tense story of the Cuban missile crisis, "So, gentlemen, what are we going to do now?"

Thirty is a good number, else I will blow a valve. I stop at 30, since to go to 31 would bring further stress, high blood pressures, rashes or boils. Stress: it, especially, visits us now. So, to combat it, I teach myself to act like a submarine commander, one whose vessel is constantly stalked by stinky, wayward Soviets wishing to fire torpedos. I had a friend like that once; he actually <u>liked</u> the anxiety. He embraced it. I must remake myself into him. Morph. Eventually, this battle for the hearts and minds of Americans, most, will be entered into and won, but it will not be easy and it will not be short. In the meantime, prepare for the battle.

* * *

Part of our money difficulties was terse bad luck. Unbeknownst to us at the time, and as happened to many others, we had become enveloped in a perfect storm. The expression is: To be Down on One's Luck. "As good luck would have it," did not occur to us (William Shakespeare, <u>The</u> <u>Merry</u> <u>Wives</u> <u>of</u> <u>Windsor</u>. Act III, Scene 5, Line 77). Sophocles writes, "The friends of the unlucky are far away (Unknown drama. <u>L'argument</u> 773). But, then again, perhaps it is true, as Ralph Waldo Emerson writes, that only "Shallow men believe in luck." (<u>Conduct</u> <u>of</u> <u>Life</u> <u>Worship</u>). In any case, what were the trinity of unhappy circumstances that gave rise to this most unwelcome yet perfect storm?

Three forces were arrayed and, when gathered together, they gained an extra strength, exponential's energy, a compounding momentum. They were:

1. The inability to sell our Vermont home. Our reasonable, but absolutely false, assumption had been in April of 2007 that we would sell our Vermont home, roughly breaking even on it, and that we would immediately use that considerable equity received to pay down debt. We had planned to do what millions of other families

had already accomplished: Yet, we thought like Custer, poorly. Alas, alack, alarkaday, <u>on</u> <u>that</u> <u>very</u> <u>same</u> <u>month</u> the housing market began to soften and then to collapse. Why? In all but four states (Florida, California, Nevada, and Arizona - where rampant speculation, encouraged <u>for</u> <u>decades</u> by overly "enthusiastic," (re: greedy) realtors pushing for an always greener surfeit, burst), the housing market collapsed because the <u>overall</u> <u>economy</u>, for all the various, sundry reasons already mentioned, tanked. To be very clear, the 2008 meltdown, caused by greedy under-regulated financial institutions, <u>in</u> <u>turn</u>, made the housing market fall. By and large, houses were not overpriced.

2. In building our New York home, we went over budget by 10%, which is not too bad. Nearly all builders around here use Time & Materials (T and M), rather than fixed quotes. If the builder is unfocused or unethical, T and M is a license to print money. In March of 2007, I asked our contractor how much money it would take to complete our project, a dream home which we hoped would be in our children's hands forever. He said, "X dollars." By the time we finally asked him to leave that summer, the remaining total had risen to 4X or nearly 5X. This last increment put us deeply into trouble. Also, it must be mentioned (since to omit is a graver fault: "By telling of it, made such a sinner of his memory, to credit his own lie," (William Shakespeare. <u>The</u> <u>Tempest</u>. Act I, Scene 2, Line 100) that many of the men he had "working" for him engaged on the jobsite, while we were

paying them upwards of $40.00 per hour, in the relaxing, yet confusing, smoking of marijuana. One Monday morning, for instance, only a little after 6 AM, I discovered six or seven of these "gentlemen of nirvana" smoking hard at the aromatic weed: Yesca! To kick off the day! Drowning men clutch at straws! They, not unkindly, offered me some, but, I, starting to boil, declined. I immediately called their boss to demur; he said that there was nothing that he could do since they all do it. A poor excuse, or not one at all. I argued that such smoking would result in many errors of workmanship and rampant forgetfulness, and, pray tell, crest overruns. Can one imagine? Not long afterwards we asked them all to take the pot smoking party elsewhere, but, by then, the horse was already out of the barn, or, as is also sometimes said, the patient was already in the hospital, unconscious and deep in intensive care.

Ought I to have taken keener care to watch and guard their productivity? Yes. Yes, yet, their decline of efficiency was gradual and only slowly increased. Bit by bit, and at first hard to see, like a house whose paint only slowly begins to fade and peel, by slivered negative changes, they became lazy and lazier. Risky financial entities mushroomed at the same time as our debt, driven by excessive spending, rose. Absent any boss's protest, ought I to have yelled, remonstrated? What lazy man calls himself lazy? Soon, we "got out of harm's way," (Miguel de Cervantes, Don Quixote. Part I, Chapter 6. P. 130) but by then, kind reader, shellbacks, ye old salt sailors all, the damage was done and the ship, well, she of once stout rowan timber and the captain's finest rare flame mahogany, she was taking on great and uncountable volumes of water. And, as Will says again: "Things past redress are now with me past care." (William Shakespeare. <u>King Richard II</u>. Act II, Scene 3, Line 171).

Now I see with a backward glance (which is usually the one more true) that in becoming the friend of the builder I had made a mistake. I well knew this lesson before but, over time, unlearnt it. Then, I had not had a prayer in hell of retaining any objectivity. Blinders. This was my mistake for which I am fully culpable. Now, we will all bear the brunt.

For instance, in a normal business relationship, in which friendship does not occlude one's vision, if I had witnessed even one incident of marijuana smoking, immediately the entire crew would have been kicked off the job, all protests notwithstanding; the lazers would have been 86'd!

Too, over the years of construction, I sent to the builder hundreds of faxes: To clarify, to question, to complain, as one does; any customer has the right to get these faxes answered quickly. However, increasingly, they were ignored, scores of them. For example, faxes regarding our generator, which did not work for three months, were mostly neglected. Similarly, then, after 1 or 2 of any of these faxes were not answered in a round pace, I should have told the whole crew to depart. Goodbye, Gladys. Depart. It was my fault not to stop this gravy train more quickly. Any friendship makes for a softer head.

3. To conclude this unholy trinity, we must touch upon the crash of the stock market in 2008: Its value went from a high of 14,000 points down, nearly, to 7,000, a decline of almost half. I have seen this figure for percentage lost that year: 41. Yet: Should this not have been foreseen? Given the <u>dozens</u> of intrinsically destabilizing entities put in place by the virtually uncontrolled financial institutions themselves, might this crash not have been foretold? What good are all those degrees from places like Wharton School of Business if they do not give to their recipients the perspicacity or cleverness to predict such a slump? People like Paul Volcker (see this chapter's beginning epigram) and Meredith Whitney were mostly routinely scoffed at, so grand was the hubris, so fully developed the machismo. William D. Cohen quotes the truth-telling Whitney in his book, <u>House</u> <u>of</u> <u>Cards</u>:

"We believe those lenders with exposure to this segment (largely subprime lenders) will experience lose levels of great enough enormity to not only substantially erode profitability but which would also impale capital positions." (P.301)

How correct she was, but mostly disregarded. Indeed, in some quarters she was made fun of, her castigators using pejorative words like "dire", or "grim".

Because of the markets' precipitous fall, we experienced 3 margin calls, meaning that many of our stocks had to be sold to more properly collaterize our loan (which was higher than it should have been due to #1 and #2 above). These sell-offs hugely confirmed losses, and further, they resulted in a disastrous cash position. Overnight, our rapidly declining trust was frozen by the Bank. Suddenly, or at least so it seemed, we had no cash flow to speak of, none at all.

Is this attentive banking? Did anyone at the Bank ever say, baldly, clearly, "Stop. You are on the edge of trouble!" No. Nobody said that because they always believed (almost in a frantic crazed, or religious sort of way) that the market would <u>never</u> turn sharply south. These brainwashed men thought that they, like gods, could read the future! Among them, if there were cynics or detractors, we never heard much from them. We mostly head from yes men, sycophants, those wearing rose colored spectacle. (I will address the question of our responsibility more fully in Chapter #7.) I speculate that any voices of dissent were squelched, or, worse, that their words of restraint were laughed at for their lack of aggressiveness and unwillingness to take always greater risks. Even as the market tanked our experts spoke of the tantalizing value of derivatives: To whom? These great, get-rich schemes remind me of the gold fever at Deadwood Gulch in the Dakota Territory in 1876. Wild Bill Hickok was there at my shoulder saying: History repeats itself.

So, we had taken too many risks and paid for that bad habit dearly. During that long, cold winter of 2008-2009 sometimes we could not buy milk for the kids. Like many we started to conserve like never before. The challenge became, as William Thackery writes, "How to live well on nothing a year." (<u>Vanity Fair</u>, 1847-1848). Nearly all items, small and large, were put up for sale, but all sold poorly or at a large lose (confirming, once again, asset depreciation), since thousands of potential buyers had similarly been hard hit by the 2008 crash, and they, therefore, simply lacked much <u>discretionary</u> cash. Instead of something selling for 2x, it sold for 1x, and we were not unhappy to take it. To eat and, simply, to endure, became central, predominant. Shakespeare, in <u>Troilus</u> <u>and</u> <u>Cressida</u>, speaks of "Appetite, a universal wolf" (I.3.121). The lean animal stood alert at our door, looking upward to our faces with the hungriest of eyes.

So, we struggled onward, lurching, tottering, helped mostly by prayer, close friends, and a smattering of thoughtful relatives. All was on sale, including both our homes, furniture, artifacts of all kinds, cars, boats, tractors, snow-blowers, copper pans, almost full tubes of toothpaste and any unused razor blades. Ha! Those last two items are an exaggeration, another example of my Irish inclination to stretch the truth. It is a little joke and one sorely needed. We started to buy "Poor-Boy" brand Romaine lettuce only due to its lower price. We stopped going out to eat, entirely, curtailed nearly all magazine subscriptions, and purchased only plonk, never fine bottles of Bordeaux or Chianti: To drink deeply became a kind of modest salve, a lead to a deeper sleep, one where, for a time, deep in the land of Nod, I did not see the wolf, licking his chops, eyeing us hungrily, lustfully, with derision. We bought only tough shoulder cuts of meat, tons of fruits and vegetables but only those in season, and avoided most pre-packaged foods. We became, inexorably, "as cheap as stinking mackerel" (William Shakespeare, <u>King</u> <u>Henry</u> <u>IV</u> <u>Part</u> <u>I</u>. Act II, Scene 4, Line 357), and adopted as a challenging dictum that line from somewhere, "It is fun to be frugal. Fun, don't you see it, Leona, fun!"

Slowly things began to brighten. A car here, a bauble there, were sold. We moved out of the main house in New York and, thus, were able to rent it on a weekly basis to folks, alternatively, either careful or not with our treasure. I sold a tractor, purchased for $12,000 for $7,800 and considered myself doggoned lucky. Thermostats went down to 55°F and sweaters came on. Time passed a bit more easily and some of the anguish and anxiety and strain of endless worry about money ("How are we to pay that bill?" "What about all those other ones that prodigiously loom?") began to dissipate.

Right after the turn of the year, I cashed in my Individual Retirement Account (IRA), an act which carries with it extreme penalties and taxes but which was necessitated by our impossible cash flow situation. But, here is the key: I had mistakenly given to the Bank my IRA for safe-keeping. Those eager legions had promised constant, proud appreciation. Of course, this had not taken place! Once again, they had not done their job! I had handed it to them 10 years ago at 5x and they had returned it to me at 3.5x. Idiots! Hornswogglers! Snow jobbers! I would have been better off putting it in a sock or an empty coffee can in the backyard. Finaglers! Cheese-eaters! But, as Billy Wilder, and many others, says: "Hindsight is always 20/20." (John Robert Colombo, ed. <u>Colombo's</u> <u>Hollywood</u>, Collins, P. 79).

* * *

It took perhaps a week for the cashing in of the IRA to settle. All involved knew, or should have known, had they been awake and not asleep when this matter was discussed, that soon, within a matter of a day or two, that considerable sums of monies from it would be deposited in our checking account, whereby bills, e.g., a mortgage, might be paid. Our

Vermont mortgage was due January 3, 2009 and since the funds did not hit until January 6, 2009, technically, we were in default. Overnight, on the close of business on the 3rd, we lost all our proper credit, and, to date, that rating has not yet been restored. Today, therefore, we could not get financing to buy a used, $5000.00 pickup truck. Remember?

Maybe the Bank does not like us because of the acerb, derisive tone of the many letters and faxes that I have sent to them. Indeed, these gentlemen still seem to act proudly about the job that they have done for us, for many. My stridency and bitterness... perhaps they have been the wrong tack. Are they, again I ask myself, too strident and bitter? Perhaps, so close to the forest, I cannot see the trees. Shortly will follow further compositions grounded in even sharper astringencies so that the reader might judge for himself whether they are extreme.

Yet, it is important to be able to speak. Often, in argument, I asked one of the minions, these improvident deliverers of doom, if I might speak. I would ask him, archly, "Must I be silent? May I disagree? Do I have your permission to think differently?" Perhaps I have scarred them rash to our disservice. Maybe the verbal receiver at the bank says, "These words are razors to my wounded heart." (William Shakespeare, <u>Titus Andronicus,</u> Act I, Scene I, 315). Yet, again, might I have been more the healer, and less the surgeon, drawing to the bone, and if so, where would we be? Better off? Or Worse?

All told, I have not meant to skewer them, these bankers, however much it may appear; but, rather, to make clear their still thriving power, their still growing insulation, their still prospering club whose members are not the least touched by trouble or doubt. Truth said, that which has happened to our little ship of 5 has likewise occurred to millions of others like us who, too, have witnessed their net worth drop from, say, 4x to 1x. Passing muster, these comments are not meant to be solely castigatory, but illustrative of a broader issue: That the banks have too much, and a still expanding, power; and that, concomitantly, a sleeping nation whose job it must be to rein in these rampant and driving forces, must awaken herself if she is to be happily returned to all her people and not just a select few garnered together by such an ascending power.

***

What follows, then, is a mostly chronological series of letters to the ersatz leaders our Bank, with nearly all of them composed in a fierce anger engendered by the greatest worry since on many of the days in question, as stated earlier, we could not buy milk for the children.

By the way, especially for all those who doubt it (including you, Thomas) some of the names have been tamed or tainted or tangled or teased or thrown down or tranquilized to protect the trifling tinpots from themselves. Today, they will call them trumped up charges, Don, trillby attempts at tlac talk by someone who has lost his marbles, but, what the tack hammer, somebody needs to talk, and this is not twoddle. Why not, Tony, have it be said by a no sugarcoat tiger who took it on the chin?

***

A short military aside: In the same way, fiddling its fingers, the American Army sat around 60 miles west of Berlin, doing not much for that month of April, 1945, allowing the Russians to seize the city, rape the women, plunder the endless and stolen riches of the Reich. Sat around...

Dear Mr. Phil N. Ditcher,   10/7/08

Yesterday, we heard that the Bank is using $8 Billion to re-write _____ loans at a lower principal and lower interest rate level. That is a smart and decent move. Would that sort of thing be possible for our NY mortgage?

Thanks,

DM

P.S. The amoral and reckless fellows responsible for this mess ought to be arrested, tried, and then skinned!

Dear Mr. Phil N. Ditcher,   10/16/08

Because underwriting standards were weakened going all the way back to the early 90s, probably in an attempt to increase home ownership among minorities and the less affluent, i.e., to gather votes, we now face a financial train wreck.[17] Everything is frozen. Many forecasters predict a long and possibly deep recession; perhaps the housing sector is bottoming now or perhaps not. It will likely not return to health until 2010, 2 years from now and therein lies the problem.

Like many people we spent too much on our home construction, say nearly 10% of total construction cost. Our home in Vermont, appraised at 2X and in which we have approximately X equity, has not sold since it was first put on the market in April 2007. (We are now attempting to rent it to slow the bleeding.) So, we have 3 major debt areas, the Vermont mortgage, the New York mortgage, and

---

17   See Stan J. Lebowitz's article "Anatomy of a Train Wreck" in the Oct. 20 issue of the National Review

the line-of-credit. Just at the time when we need maximum performance from our equities, they have, due to the train wreck caused by gambling and unscrupulous bankers, tumbled badly. We have lost a fortune in the stock market, probably 2X. Let us recall: First, there was the slide in 2000-2001 and now this much deeper crash. I would bet that our total average rate of return, <u>not</u> considering the recent crash, is <u>less</u> than that for bonds, say 4%.

Considering that salient fact, I suggest that the Bank might want to reconsider our 2 mortgage rates, something that would be not only good business nationally but also allow us to keep our house here in Tupper Lake. I note that the Bank had taken the absorbed "Blank's" home loans and quickly reduced <u>both</u> their principal amounts and rates. As I suggest, this is good business <u>and</u> allows people to keep their homes. If the Bank were to lower our interest rates from 6% to 4%, it would allow us to take less from our trust every month, thus not depleting the main income source. Knowing that we have been solid Private Bank customers for 10 years, that I have been banking with the Bank personally since at least 1972, and that I used to deposit checks for my now deceased dad in the 1950s, perhaps will allow you to appreciate our loyalty.

These times require innovative measures that not long ago could not have been foretold. Should a few thousand greedy banks, essentially unregulated and engendering financial products that no one really understands, be allowed to force foreclosures across the country? Thus, the dream of home ownership is swiftly truncated. Also, escalating property taxes and home insurance rates are forcing homeowners to wonder if it is worth it: To own a house. Many may say: I would rather rent! Therefore, unless drastic measures are taken soon, the U.S. financial industry stands on the edge of turning what was once a family's main asset, its home, into a nuisance or obvious liability. For now, we wish to stay here. We both are working hard, to close the gap. Let us work together on this problem, which admittedly and as already stated, we had a hand in creating.

One good thing has happened to us: We are learning to live more frugally now. Secondly, fewer people will work in financial services and this is also a good thing. I remember back to the 60s when my dad told me, a non-listening teenager, that too many people were "on the boob." How correct he was and look where that surfeit has got us all!

Kind regards,

DM

Dear Phil N. Ditcher,   10/30/09

Because of you unethical and unnecessary margin calls, we are out of cash: Our credit card is maxed out, our trust is frozen and our checking account is frozen, as well. When you made those foolish calls, we had already realized that we could not longer afford this house. Now, it is on the market for _____. Here's what we need:

1. Reverse all finance charges from both our credit card and the MRA.
2. Allow a temporary small extensions on our credit card so that we can use it <u>today</u> to buy gas and groceries. We live 10 miles from town and therefore, unless you do this <u>today</u>, we cannot move. Both of these are reasonable requests.

Today you will receive $20,000 from a relative: Friday, 1/2/09, liquidate my IRA and apply it to the MRA. Finally, then, apply $5,000 to the credit card. Email your response to martins@wildblue.net since our phone/fax lines are dead.

DM

Dear Ms. Kay Guerra,   11/25/08

1. I will be traveling later this week to Chicago and Michigan so please keep our credit card open.
2. What are the fees that the Bank has collected for 2008? Please fax with the total.
3. Where is the letter of apology from Daniel Lord to us for missing our appointment and implying that I am stupid. Also, we want to see proof that that letter has gone to Dr. Peak Woo and that it is part of his permanent employee record.
4. I want you to determine the losses that our account suffered because of the 3 margin calls in the last 3 months. I want you to make these calculations based on a reasonable Dow of 12,500. I want them done on an individual fund basis, calculated for each call and then totaled. I want you to fax the results here in a week.

                                                        DM

Dominic M. Martin

Dear Mr. Phil N Ditcher,

Let us look backward for a moment. When we, and others, lost many thousands of dollars in the early part of this decade, was there not someone in the organization who correctly forecasted the popping of the technologic bubble? What was the source of that neglect?

The Fannie Mae and Freddie Mac loosening of rules? Did it not have a political catalyst? That is, to get more people to vote for Clinton?

The programmed and block trading — How could anyone think that they would benefit the little guy? — that is, the average American investor who has lost more than most this past quarter.

Hedge funds — how could they ever work well over time? Did not some banks look with embarrassment at the ludicrous fees their managers took from them? These banks that sat on their hands — Do they not share some incipient or large responsibility?

Derivatives — why is it a good idea to sell a mortgage to a 3rd party?: The one entity can never know the other. Should we all not have known that this was not a good idea?

And, thus, a house of cards was erected. Not by us. Was there not a single expert or a keen lone wolf among you who might have urged caution or restraint? Yet, would he not have been ignored? Wall Street's greed and government's inattention (including <u>not</u> enforcing existing statutes (re: Barney Frank)) combined to force this financial collapse, a collapse which has, of course, affected the average American family in a much more fundamental way than the entities, the banks and other financial interests, that engendered them. Is that fair? Does "fair" matter anymore? To Whom?

To give a fix: Eliminate hedge funs, derivatives, programmed and block trading of all kinds. <u>Completely</u>

nationalize, for the time being, Freddie Mac and Fannie Mae. Fire Chris Cox of the SEC and prosecute all guilty of fraud: Tough to do, but it all can be done.

What has the bank done for us? Lost us a bundle 2 times, once in the early decade by neglecting to predict the tech collapse (I urged a move to bonds but was constantly ignored), and secondly, in this quarter, by the bank's inability to predict, and therefore, avoid, this present financial collapse. Could it not have been foreseen? But, was not the essential source of this neglect, greed?

My IRA, had it been invested in bonds 10 years ago, would be worth 2 times what it is today. Pitiful! Ivory domes! Gutbuckets!

Our children's educational trusts have also performed listlessly. We would have been smarter to put them in bonds and forget about them. Five percent is better than a flat performance.

We have been caught in a perfect storm, the simultaneous coincidence of 3 factors:

a) not selling our Vermont house

b) spending 10% more than we should have on Tupper Lake

c) the financial collapse aforementioned

This collapse has led to our not being able to sell our Vermont house, so A and C are linked. All the while, even while the bank has been losing money for us, or performing at a very poor rate, we have paid fees to it, and I ask: How can this be justified? I suggest that one outcome of this collapse will be that, from now on, eventually, fees will be indexed to performance. What a novel idea: The Bank only makes money when the customer makes money. Perhaps, there will be more attention to detail and less speculation and empty forecasting.

Now that we are listing our house for sale — where are the experts? To what safe office have they retreated?

We own "blank" dollars in real estate. Why was that fact not considered when the 3 margin calls were made? We insist that a calculation be made as to what those margin calls cost us, based on a Dow of 12,500, and that that amount be deducted from the line-of-credit. Those margin calls were unnecessary and unethical, as I'm sure you know. Though legal, they clearly point to the fact that the Bank is not interested primarily in the customers' welfare. Here's the deal: If the Bank had spent as much careful time making money for us as it did in making the margin calls, they would not have been necessary. Did the Martin family invent hedge funds or derivatives, did we loosen the mortgage rules, and did we start programmed trading? I thought it was the banks that did those things, watched over by a sleepy government? Why should we have to pay for their endless greed?

DM

(12/1/08)

P.S. Again, where is the letter of apology from Lord? Still, we stand neglected.

P.S.S. As Branch Rickey said of Leo Durocher, the Bank "had an infinite capacity to go into a bad situation and make it worse." Thank you, Mr. Roger Kahn. HA!

Dear Ms. Kay Guerra,
AKA, Doña Bosco,   12/12/08

Beware the marketing types, the back slappers, all those that are, even occasionally, excessively jocular. They work less and earn [sic] more. They do not know what it is to wake up hours before the sun and work all day without stopping to eat because the job will not wait. Instead, they will have all this extra time to wait, to plot, to scheme. Flatassers, connivers, slick-WIllies. Sadly, they have secured our nation for themselves.

DON'T FORGET!: Sell my IRA and put all proceeds in our checking account. <u>Fax</u> to me the total. When I turned that over to you folks nearly 10 years ago, it was worth much more. Why did you not put it in bonds? Then, today, it would have been worth nearly double. No: Once more the bank "knew better". Clearly, the bank's performance has been despicable, I complained about this <u>many</u> <u>times</u> and was <u>ignored.</u>

While I am at it, some sage advice (again):

1.   Get rid of hedge funds
2.   Get rid of all programmed and block trading
3.   Get rid of all derivatives or other entities wherein loans can be re-packaged and re-sold
4.   Privatize Fannie Mae and Freddie Mac. Sue the people who have been in charge and prosecute them for fraud.

In short, unless banks and Wall Street make it a place where the average, small investor can make a return better than bonds, <u>you</u> <u>will</u> <u>not</u> <u>have</u> <u>a</u> <u>business</u>. Eliminate all schemes that appeal only to the wheeler-dealer day trader, because his goals are <u>intrinsically</u> <u>counter</u> to those of the American, average Joe. Some "financial advisers" are getting paid large sum's for generating this same advice. <u>Don't</u> take the counsel of those who only stand to benefit and who got us all in this mess in the first place.

On another matter, I remind you again that Mr. Lord 1) missed our meeting inexcusably, and 2) suggested that if I were not smart enough to understand margin calls that I should talk to a math teacher at my college who could more patiently explain them to me. Hubris! Arrogance! Who do you people think you are?: Nobles? Lords? Prince who can do no wrong? For clarification on this issue: Ask Mr. Ditcher: He was on the line! Mr. Lord's comment was snide, rude, and unprofessional. I am due a written apology and will continue to demand one.

Doña Bosco: What did they teach you there? Can anyone, amongst you pack of unseeing drones, apologize? Shameless! The nation stands at war, with you.

DM

Dear Ms. Kay Guerra,
AKA Doña Bosco,   1/16/09

Given the fact that the Bank is receiving $45 Billion from the taxpayer, it ought to:

1. Cut our 2 mortgages immediately by 2%, from 6% to 4%, together with no fees or points of any kind.
2. Return the roughly _____ taken from our trust by the unnecessary and unethical margin call of 2 months ago.

It is time for the Bank to do the <u>right</u> <u>thing</u>.

DM

Dominic M. Martin

Dear Ms. Kay Guerra,
AKA Doña Bosca,   2/21/09

I am sure that given what the president said in Mesa, Arizona
last week that you have already thoughtfully considered
how his new federal programs, to lower interest rates on
home mortgages as well as on the principal amounts, (two
things that we proposed to you <u>months</u> <u>ago</u>) might help
our family. Please investigate and report back. If there is a
program available, even though both our houses are for sale,
we would like to avail ourselves of it.

Sincerely,

DM

P.S. You are presiding over, if not encouraging and abetting,
a drastic diminution of our family's wealth. Just so there is
no doubt.

Dear Mr. Herry Barker,   2/20/09

In 2001-2, repeatedly, I told the Bank specifically, Mr.
Tom Long, (one of a long series of managers — this was a
revolving door!), to sell our equities, especially tech stocks,
but, as usual, we were ignored. At that time the NASDAQ
was dropping from its high of 4500 to what it is today,
.1600. Always, the managers said that they were the experts
and that they knew better. Obviously, this was, and is not,
the case. Let me remind you, tersely, of what Ms. Jane
Bryant Quinn, <u>Newsweek</u> columnist, says of stock market
predictors: "Half of them don't know what's going to happen
tomorrow and the other half don't know they don't know."
(<u>CNN</u> April 4, 1994) True experts would have predicted
this "tech bubble" and bought bonds as a protective move;
however, since they are not the experts that they purport to
be, no action was taken and we lost on the order of x. Note:
This is separate from the <u>larger</u> <u>debacle</u> of 2008.

DM

Mr. Phil N. Ditcher,   3/25/09

Last night, the President said that 40% of all mortgages are eligible for re-financing. For the, it must be, 5th time, can someone there please tell us whether we qualify? Federal money is available as incentives for the bank to encourage them to lower principals and rates of interest.

Further, as long as a calculation is being made regarding what rate of return the Bank has achieved in 10 years, why not also determine:

a)   the total fees that we have paid the bank in that some decade

b)   the amount snatched out of the Martin family wallet under the margin call of last Fall.

The calculation should be based upon a "normal" DOW of 12,500.

If these calculations are made, we all will have a full, that is, not one-sided view, of both sides of the nickel. By the way, how much have we lost since the Bank has historically been unable to retain good managers, e.g. Mr. Tom Snow?

Yet, the fundamental question will remain:

Not, "What have you gone in the past?", but rather, "What are you now prepared to do?"

Sincerely,

DM

Dear Mr. Herry Barker,   3/1/09

It would be funny, were it not so disheartening, for Kate and I to recall that one year ago, before the unethical and needless margin calls which took x from our trust, we were paying all of our bills rather easily.

DM

Dear Mr. Phil N. Ditcher,   3/23/09

We do not understand why some small, monthly cash transfers from our trust cannot be made as long as proportionate line of credit payments are made simultaneously. In that case, the bank's position, and ours, with respect to the loan/cash ratios, would be the same.

The federal government has authorized $75 Billion dollars for people in our position, that is, for those who are having a difficult time making mortgage payments. <u>For months,</u> I have been asking the Bank to investigate whether we would qualify for these programs. If the Bank receives an incentive, i.e., cash, to lower principal or interest rates, why is it so automatically opposed to such a proposition? Such intransigence is neither helpful nor very business-like. Will someone please investigate, and pray tell, respond?

Regarding the mortgage payments, we propose that both be cut in half in time for the May 3 and 5 automatic deductions from our MRA account. This is a reasonable request. Because of how badly the financial institutions (not just the Bank) have damaged the economy, it could well be <u>many years</u> before home buying liquidity for most people returns. People simply do not have the money that they used to have, which is no wonder since, because of Wall Street's greedy excesses, the housing market has lost half its value up the chimney. One must ask if the Bank wishes to own two far-flung properties, pay our excessive property taxes, high insurance and extravagant heating bills. This scheme would allow us to continue to make the two mortgage payments and preclude the Bank from owning two properties that it, no doubt, does not wish to own.

Just so you know that we are not sitting on our hands, as of June 1, we are moving into the guest house so that we can rent the main house for x/ week. We hope to make x this summer by this rental. This was a quick, pro-active decision on our part which demonstrates that we realize the extreme gravity of our financial situation. However, it should be noted that because of what the financial institutions (not just the Bank) have done, <u>all</u> assets sold fetch roughly 50¢ on the dollar. Have I not mentioned before, the phrase "<u>confirming</u> <u>losses</u>"? For example, our wooden boat, which we paid a fair $2x$ for, may sell this Spring for $1x$ because the market is so poor. Does the Bank not understand that this is exactly how wealth continues to erode?

Nonetheless, we will continue to try to sell assets a decent, not great, price. Yesterday, we sold a tractor for $7800, but one purchased for $12,000.

Further, this past week Edward and I went to the mid-Atlantic states for job interviews, both for teaching positions and in the wine business. I have been offered a job in Virginia for _____, starting June 1 and am in the process of final negotiations for that position. We will keep you informed. Clearly, this search, once again, demonstrates how quickly and pro-actively we are trying to get out of the hole.

Finally, regarding the rate of return, two things need to be said:

1. The only reason to invest in equities is to gain a return of 7% or above, otherwise, one might as well be happy with the 5% that bonds generate. I do not believe that the Bank has achieved an average return of 7%, especially in 2001-2 and this year when the market has lost huge values. Given the tech bubble (which was bound to pop) and today's toxic climate (a fragile house of cards which finally fell), why were these 2 collapses not foretold by you, the experts? Perhaps they were not so smart after all — May I say so or should I be quiet?

2. Improper securitization. It should be illegal for banks to package and sell off loans to a 3rd party. Unless this practice is gotten rid of, Wall Street will remain toxic. The financial wheeler-dealers who have put us in this pickle should be required to go out and get a real and productive job, one that helps, and does not hurt, <u>all</u> Americans. As my late and much-missed father used to say, "There are too many guys, my young son, on the boob!"

DM

P.S. Imagine, Buster, that this word is going to get out and it will not be good for you. So, imagine that: More trouble ahead!

Dear Ms. Kay Guerra,   4/1/09

Bankers used to be the most cautious and prudent types, disinclined to gamble or be reckless with anyone's money, let alone a client's.

For at least the last 2 decades, caution and prudence have morphed to gambling and recklessness, yet most bankers will not suffer from these inexcusable, yet expected, losses. Indeed, the high pay, fees and Christmas bonuses roll on, while the average American has to fend for himself. Shall he ever trust the banker again?

And, what about the horrendous losses our three children's 529 plans have suffered? What about those, or is it somehow, too easy to forget?

DM

Dear Mr. Daniel Lord,   4/1/09

Our family needs another margin call like we need a root canal for a bad tooth. It used to be that bankers thought about: "What is the right thing to do?" Now it is: "Do we have a legal basis for this action?" Or, "Does the Bank have any legal liability?" I promise you that we are doing everything we can to right the ship, but notices like this one do not help — I believe the phrase is "Confirming Losses." For 5 or 6 months, we have asked for help with lowering the interest and principal on our two mortgages. What is to happen?

DM

Dear Mr. Daniel Lord,   4/3/09

Since we cannot rely on regulations we must rely on honorable men to make the right decisions, to speak up clearly when they see something, like derivatives backed by toxic mortgages, blowing their whistles to their bosses who will probably just ignore them. If someone had spoken out more loudly when intrinsically destabilizing entities were established, might not this fiasco, this casino, been avoided? Did they think too much of the fees they might accrue, rather than the deleterious effects on the average American family who had done nothing to create them?

Why were such dangerous financial entitities engendered? Perhaps it is this: Mid-level financiers had to justify to their bosses their increasingly high salaries and bonuses. Meetings, that constant stock-in-trade, in which positions were sanctified and of stations made clear, that ultimate time-wasting and self-justified exercise for all time, for all those wearing a white collar, had to be scheduled, and there, then, that foolish seduction by the testosterone-ridden young of their inherently more cautions elders, that sad seduction began. It was not the quintessential hard sell. The cautious fell quickly into line. Those with the corner office very high up did not much worry about the dangerous details as long as considerable fees could be billed for doing very little. That would help, temporarily, the bottom line. And thus, over time and the promise of always higher rates of return, common sense began to drift away.

At the same time, due to the excessively close relationships that exists between the financial industry (if that is, indeed, the word) and the federal government, regulations that might have governed, controlled, or eliminated these new or emerging financial mechanisms were either rescinded or ignored. To wit, Representative Phil Gramm of Texas actively encouraged de-regulation of the financial system. Also, anti-trust laws that would have, for example, prevented the Bank's absorption of _____, were ignored. We now have the expression "Too Big To Fail." Unfortunately, what has fallen is the pocketbook of the average American and what have been forever decimated are the savings of the average older American. I ask you today: Was it worth it?

DM

Dear Ms. Kay Guerra,   5/27/09

Sometime today the payment due on the line of credit will take place, nearly cleaning out our checking account; shortly after that event, we will not be able to buy milk for our children. And to think that a year ago, before the unnecessary and unethical margin call, we were able to pay all our bills, albeit closely. Do you feel any small tug of guilt for your large part in this painful case?

Because of the financial meltdown engendered by greedy banks and a somnolent government, our daughter's modeling career is stagnant, my full-time position at _____ College was eliminated by the president there; further, my wife's position at the grammar school was cut. Additionally, we are not even receiving any offers (at 50¢/ dollar!) on disposable assets. Shortly, we shall move out of the main house so that we might rent it, but the two websites where we have it proudly listed are very quiet. A house that might have rented for $6000/ week now goes for $1500. Perhaps you do not fully grasp the extent to which people have lost <u>cash</u>.

All over we have creditors screaming at us: Propane suppliers, insurance providers, electric companies. Every day our credit is further harmed. We have decided, as you know, to sell both our Vermont and New York homes, yet, things are slow, and, in the meantime, we need your help. Once again, we ask for your assistance — a reduction of both our mortgages and their interest rates. Secondly, we need some money to pay our other bills. Frankly, we need at least $15,000 today to get back even until summer rental income arrives. Sir, this is the right and proper thing to do.

Sincerely,

DM

P.S. I continue to apply for work all over the eastern U.S. So far, because of the economy, no luck. Will not give up.

Dear Mr. Herry Barker,   6/1/09

Good morning.

I hope that you will make the case to whomever will listen that, throughout, we took the financial advice, now known as seriously flawed, from the Certified Financial Advisors of the Bank. It was <u>their</u> idea to engender a line of credit secured by our family's trust. It was <u>their</u> idea to set the upper limit of that line way too high, which resulted in margin calls, once the market turned south, and in turn, our not being able to pay our bills today. We never <u>proposed</u> anything but rather were <u>proposed to.</u> We were never expressly warned, so hell-bent was the Bank to lend money in those now halcyon days; and, in fact, our plan: To pay down the line from the sale of Vermont, was <u>praised</u> as most responsible, if not shrewd. We never had any other bank advising us about the line of credit. Since we only took the Bank's advice and listened carefully to their most senior advisors, does not the Bank owe us greatly, if, indeed, this is a relationship of shared, not single, responsibilities? Does anyone know the definition of the word: Fiduciary?: of or pertaining to a trust; that is, something relating to a 2-way, not 1-way, street?

My father told me early on about the triangle — blaming it on the guy not in the room, to both evade responsibility and gain advantage. When we last spoke, you referred to the people you speak to who are deciding our fate in somewhat similar language, which to me is most worrisome. It is a good thing my father, Ed Martin, who co-founded the American Commercial Bank in Ventura, California, is no longer with us to witness the excessive lending, the flawed instruments like derivatives, the neglect of the anti-trust laws, and this constant use of the triangle. He would be more than appalled. Markings of treachery and

121

an unbounded arrogance. By the way, my mother, Florence Martin, knew _____, whose husband co-founded the Bank of _____, which became the bank you work for today. Perhaps I should point that out to the fellows in Santa Barbara: An ironic circle is thus completed.

One piece of good news: We may have our boat sold. If that happens we would get two months of easy breathing. With your help, we need <u>TIME</u>. Our aim is to get out of the Northeast as soon as possible.

Sincerely,

DM

Dear Mr. Herry Barker,   6/18/09

Yesterday the President spoke about the financial world's culture of irresponsibility and how the government must step in as a greater regulator because the banks have not. I hope that you, and many listless others there at the Bank realize that what the president said yesterday — that greedy, unregulated excesses in the banking industry led to the financial meltdown — duplicate exactly what I have been saying since last Fall. So, if I say it, I am ignored or called a crackpot; but, if President Obama says it, he is called prescient or a seer. His comments give credence to our ironclad case that the Bank was negligent and that our family is due sizeable financial compensation for that neglect.

DM

cc: Mr. Todd Toth, attorney

Dominic M. Martin

Dear Ms. Kay Guerra,   6/2/09

Because of the surprising, if not miraculous generosity of a friend, we are sending $10,000 to Santa Barbara. The check should be there by Friday, the 5th. Please do not foreclose on <u>either</u> of our homes, whose mortgages are due on the 3rd and the 5th.

Sincerely,

DM

Dear Ms. Kay Guerra,   10/7/09

Instead of the 3 margin calls, why did the Bank, you, not quickly take out a 2nd mortgage on our NY home where we have massive equity. Upon its sale, it would have been swiftly paid back. Such a move would have saved our family quite a bit. You could not be bothered, I guess.

Certified Financial Advisor (CFA): Isn't the real basis for the acronym

Claptrap Fudging Asses
Crum Fluke Alibi-Ikes
Cadging Freeloader Apple-heads?

How many more would you like to see? I've got plenty more, fuzzle-head. How about a nice simple one:

Crap Filthy Amateurs?

Slinkers. Tinhorns. Dopes. And, you're telling me to shut my gob? Phooey! Why?

DM

Through their carelessness, their reckless financing, their vain attempts to ingratiate themselves with a self-important client [Long Term Capital Management], the Wall Street bankers had created this fiasco together.

Roger Lowenstein
When Genius Failed, Random
House; New York 2000; p.191

Wall Street is always good at fighting the last war. But these things happen and they're big, and when they happen everybody tries to look at what happened in the previous 6 months to find someone or something to blame it on. But, in truth, it was a team effort. We all fucked up. Government. Rating Agencies. Wall Street. Commercial Banks. Regulators. Investors. Everybody.

Alan Schwartz, quoted by William D.
Cohen in House of Cards: A Tale of
Hubris and Wretched Excess on Wall
Street, Doubleday; New York; 2009;
p.450

Me, poor man, My library was dukedom large enough.

William Shakespeare, The Tempest,
Act I, Scene 2, Line 109

"You go to the police like a good American, but nothing happens."

"Can we ask them about their business? What does he have under his fingernails?"

"Leave the gun. Take the cannoli."

"You are like me, we refuse to be fools, to be puppets dancing on a string pulled by other men."
(Vito to his son, Michael)
Quotes taken from the film <u>The Godfather,</u> "<u>Il Padrone</u>", written by Mario Puzo and directed by Francis Ford Coppola, 1972.

Please recall that the motif of the Godfather Trilogy is the black-and-white, still-image of puppetry; Pawns on a string.

Puppet: an adjective, sponsored or controlled by others while professing autonomy.

Chapter Seven:
The Kids' Playpen

In reading both Cohen and Lowenstein's books, anyone can, if he so chooses, to begin to assemble a list of relatively new, intrinsically destabilizing financial entities or rules which disproportionately favor the "economic royalists" or "new nobles" who have taken hold of our economy and, therefore, our nation. As you will see, it is a long one, and I am certain that I have missed more than a few of these presumeably money making gimmicks:[18]

1. The Merton-Scholes formula
2. Revolving credit arrangements
3. Leverage "haircuts"
4. "Risk-free" arbitrage
5. Toxic mortgage-backed securities
6. Credit default swaps

---

18 Gimmick: "A supposedly secret formula or angle that assures success or at least affords an advantage in gambling; a word that insinuated itself into racing jargon in the 1950s." (Dictionary of American Slang; Edited by Wentworth and Flexner; Thomas Y. Crowell, NY 1975, p. 215)

7. Hedge funds
8. Derivatives
9. Programmed and black trading
10. Repo borrowing
11. Dishonest rating agencies also asleep at the switch
12. Artificial Liquidating
13. Repeal of the Glass-Steagall Act in 1999
14. SEC's change in net capital rule
15. SEC's elimination of the uptick rule
16. Backdating stock options

What a fine mess! "The little foolery that wise men have makes a great show." (As You Like It, William Shakespeare, I.2.86). Indeed, what a caustic show! All of these things are "Monkey" tricks, a word which Brewer's defines as "mischievous, ill-natured, or deceitful actions" (p. 750). Taken together they have imposed a whole new set of chaotic, bent, un-rules upon Wall Street; and the clever, rushed Young Turks who mostly instigated these changes and who can alter them seamlessly, again, willy-milly, at near any time, they are now free to sail their stout ship of Fools (Sebastian Brant, 1509) anywhere that they would like to. Did someone say "sheep dip?" Hear's the deal: essentially, outside the purview of a government, which remains externally asleep or quiescent, money men and women of all kind and unmodest stripe have revolutionized Wall Street, morphing it into something which more matches their pleasure and greening motive, establishing an always changing children's financial playpen where they have been, are, and will be free and unshackled to pursue nearly whatever new monied dream that they might conjure. The problem is, may I mention, that this unknown, new world is made for them, and not for us, and beneath this quick process there remains "the forgotten man at the bottom of the economic pyramid" (FDR's radio address on April 7, 1932). He is someone who can only get hurt. And I wonder: Who speaks for him?

Instead, we have a nation where elite Big Shots pull the strings. Going to the Ivy League, getting a job on Wall Street, networking and making the right connections, joining that prayer circle of faux friends (re: seneca), means that, soon, one may have access to the greatest power, which is simply the ability to control other people's lives. Essentially, such a person can become a puppeteer, someone who pulls the strings, or, what is called in The Godfather "Un pezzonovante", (literally "part of a 90 year old"), a powerful person, a bigwig in government, politics or finance. The implication in the film is that these men are, most uniformly, corrupt and that is why and how "la cosa nostra" (our thing) started: So that their family could be outside the overarching and corrupt influence of *pezzonovanti*. In the script for the film, Vito Corleone asks his son, Michael, what he believes in. Michael is silent, so Vito tells him:

"Believe in a family. Can you believe in your country? Those *pezzonovanti* of the state who decide what we shall do with our lives, who declare wars they wish us to fight in, to protect what they own. Do you want to put your fate in the hands of men whose only talent is that they tricked a bloc of people to vote for them?"[19]

Are not the manipulators of Wall Street, those that use it as their "playpen for profit", the new pezzonovanti of today, the puppeteer who run the show? It, Wall Street's combination of chaos and sponging welshers retides me, Captain Horatio Hornblower, of the stock market of 1929: It was that market's rank corruption (not dissimilar to today's) and, specifically, the ubiquitous insider trading (probably even more common today) that led to Black

---

19   The Godfather Legacy, p. 31, 159. Shooting script of The Godfather, dated March 29, 1971

Tuesday. President Roosevelt understood quickly that the place had to be cleaned up, made rid of scavengers and thieves, and so he established the Securities and Exchange Commission (SEC) in 1930 to safeguard the place and to prevent another atrocious fall in the market (how he could have let it become so dissolute is another question). As is well know, he appointed Joseph P. Kennedy, JFK's father, as its first head. Right away, sharp howls and catcalls of derision were heard; "How could you put that cheating fox in charge?" Roosevelt responded to those rife and immediate complaints by saying something along these line: "Better the fox you know than the one who is a stranger. My man knows where all the holes in the fence are."

Clearly, by extension, the SEC needs today to reinvent itself since its relationship to the Street is far too cosy. How else can anyone explain the Madoff nod-off? Mark DeCambre writes in the New York Post:

> "Wall Street's top watchdog acted more like Keystone Cops than highly paid enforcers, bungling tips and missing many chances to sniff out Ponzi schemer Bernie Madoff." (September 3, 2009, p. 35)

Yet, after making these charges, I pause on point: How can I prove these claims, that financial institutions are uniformly corrupt, that arrogance and hubris fills the vision of its leaders, that lip homage or service, verbal derivations only or insincere regards, are given to those, like me, who deign unmeekly to protest? So, let us look at a few other examples to make more obvious the chicanery.

Barbara Kiviat writes that

> "Dick Fuld [the former head of Lehman Brothers] was warned. Years before Lehman Brothers tumbled into bankruptcy, roiling markets and setting off a

string of massive bailouts, underlings informed the investment bank's CEO that Lehman should get out of real estate before the credit bubble burst. Fuld ignored them."

(Time Magazine, August 24, 2009; p. 13)

Hubris. Many others have long complained, to little avail, that the relationship between Wall Street and the government is too close. John Crudele writes:

"Over the past few years I've looked into the much-too-cozy relationship between Goldman [Sachs] and Washington. I've suggested that this Wall Street firm has been acting, in essence, as an arm of the government."

(New York Post, August 27, 2009)

Apparently, too, Goldman has exclusive "trading hurdles in which traders and analysts dole out their tips to only a handful of clients." (Mark DeCambre, New York Post, August 25, 2009; p. 29). Is this sort of intransparency acceptable? Is it good for the country? Does anyone care what is fair anymore? Is it simply: Let George do it?

Curious, too, is how computer technology, largely unchecked and unregulated, has changed the market. Forget the old fogey pap that financial advisers will tell you about long-term investing in solid companies. That was in the old days! Pete-man! Hooey! Tickled Pink! Today, "Flash orders — a feature offered by some exchanges that allows high volume traders the advantage of posting orders for up to half a second and then removing them — have drawn the ire of authorities" (Justin Fox, Time Magazine, August 25, 2009; p. 35) And why not? Is this not the very definition of churning? When one asks: "Why does the government not stop this unfair practice?", one immediately answers the question with the only obvious response, "Because it does not want to!"

But, probably, the most egregious example of corruption, collusion at the oligarchy, call it what you will (hanky-panky, jugglery, underhanded dealing, being crooked as Crawley, moohlah skimming, pulling strings, this for that, itchy palmers, goose-trappers and grifters, fiddlers, porkchopping, all those brazen-faced, or bold in a bad sense and without shame (<u>Brewer's</u>, p. 155)) (A second note, and please excuse my stretch: There are near as many words for the corrupt, as there are to describe the drunken state: Sozzled, lubricated, polluted, geezed, hammered, half-stewed, etc.) was This: What happened when the government handed out TARP funds to banks in trouble: The banks immediately wrote extravagant bonus checks to their top employees. How could this take place, using taxpayer generated funds for private gain? Why did the government not anticipate that these bonus checks would be written? Perhaps it did, but saw no cause for alarm. Disgusting, and most Americans know it!

Finally, "court-appointed receivers are reaping millions of dollars in fees and are in demand as the recession unearths many alleged frauds." (James Doran, <u>New York Post</u>, August 8, 2009; p. 39) Is this the sort of government we deserve, one full of inside deals, special treatment, completely inefficient oversight and sleepy regulation, blackguards and swindlers, those whom Shakespeare calls everywhere rogues and thieves? Why is it that those two last words are now so uncommonly said? Has the crime itself been banished or disappeared? Betrayed of trust is all around. Only baser instincts reign. And "O judgement! Though art fed to brutish beasts. And men, have lost their reason." (William Shakespeare, <u>Julius Caesar</u>; Act II, Scene 2, Line 106) Perhaps that play, a study of betrayal, of trust lost, of nasty measures commingled with the just, of how some men have a way of slowly talking themselves into doing things which should not be done, perhaps that play, it more than any other, should be required reading at all business schools, now, today!, so that the young students there, *before they become corrupt*, may study how quickly desire turns to rule, honesty to denial, the common interest to selfish gain.

It is clear, then, to all who wish to see, that financial institutions can pretty much do whatever they might wish to do. Their lieutenants say, "I wouldn't call the king my cousin" (<u>Brewer's</u>; p. 281): In other words, I could not be bettered even if I were cousin to the king. Their power is at its highest peak or apotheosis; their anointed stature and rank is that of demigods or the keenest rulers in charge of countries. Someone at Goldman Sachs, well-connected, urbane, inside the gated club, making hay by the truckwood, may step briefly down to take a government job where he will take a large paycut, but, more importantly, <u>make policy</u>. After a further time he can go back to Goldman where he will benefit from the policy change he had just initiated. Is this the kind of lazy, venal, laissez-faire regulation we ought to expect from our so-called leaders? Or are there better models, a smarter choices that we might make?

Predictably, a group so privileged and set, apart fights regulation and, indeed, goes on the hellbent offense, saying it is not needed and is, counter to capitalism's foundations. The new head of the SEC, Mary Shapiro, will no doubt be tougher than the previous and somnolent Chris Cox (he must have been afraid and intimidated by Mr. Madoff, now serving 153 years in the clink. There, by the way, I hope Madoff soon finds many special friends!). Currently, according to <u>Bloomsbury</u> she is weighing changes to margin requirements, insider trading rules and other bits of financial arcana, but one must ask, "If new rules are put in place, won't these financial wizards or vedettes simply find another, more circuitous way around them?" Since, that has been the tired history: Make a rule, create a loophole. Now that they, the financial wizards, have formed, made this inner circle, one so close to the prodigious fountain of power, let it not come as a surprise to us that they will wish to keep it, protect it, guard it, so as to better secure their own futures. Now that our economy is so out of balance, with the financial institutions having achieved remarkable profits and protected power (the two go hand-in-hand), it will not be easy to rein them in, even a little. Now that the force of such cleverness has been made manifest, it shall not be simple to wrest it away. "As proper men as ever trod upon neat's leather (William Shakespeare, <u>Julius Caesar</u>; Act I, Scene I, Line 25), the well-connected financial leaders will not be likely to simply watch this accumulated power slip away with them. As William Shakespeare says so well once again: "Not all the water in the rough rude sea can wash the balm off from an anointed king." (<u>King Richard II</u>; Act II, Scene 2, Line 54) Too often, now, we are surrounded by corsairs, pirates, those sailing high before the wind.

* * *

Three quotes for the grouser's musement:

"There are idiots. Look around."

Larry Summers
as quoted by Paul Kruzman,

"How Did Economists Get It So Wrong?", <u>New York Times Magazine</u>, August 6, 2009; p. 43

"Is everybody drunk?"

> Said by the unbald Shemp, one of the
> 3 Stooges, in the movie, <u>Disorder</u> <u>in</u>
> <u>the</u> <u>Court</u>; 1936

Despite all the calamities that have happened, even more compounding mistakes continue. Often it seems to me that the crash of 2008 has taught us nothing, absolutely nothing, since the government is still asleep. Yawners! Of course, it is! How could it ever be otherwise? Banks and other financial institutions regularly curry favor with their supposed regulators, in fact, often telling they, the government's enforcers, what to do. To stop this practice, here's an idea whose time has come: All financial entities should be prevented from giving <u>any</u> money to politicians. Further, lobbyists for banks should be equally prohibited from giving money to politicians. This would be a small start on an endless job, and truly a sisyphean task.

Still, Job's post, that bringer of bad news (<u>Brewer's</u>, p. 612) says things are still worse, or unrecognized. One must first know one's enemy since here, Clarence, is the order for any fight:

1. Recognize the enemy
2. Diagnose the problem
3. Develop a battle plan
4. Carry out the operation

With this money issue, we have not yet reached #1. I regret having to say the sorry, but this Virgil Hilts (even if he does not like his name) must speak loud and clear if our nation is ever to make an underground escape from the close prison that now envelopes us.

Banks are still undeterred, unchastened, still too prone to gamble. Jenny Anderson writes in the <u>New</u> <u>York</u> <u>Times</u>

that new, exotic investments <u>every week</u> continue to flourish, especially the packaging of life insurance policies. She writes, pointedly, that "the debacle of 2008 gave financial wizardry a bad name generally, but not on Wall Street." That state of affairs can only exist because Wall Street is a foreign universe, a nation set apart, a world unto itself, an island, like Thule, a long, six day's sailing away from the rest of us muggins. (<u>Brewer's</u>, p. 1114) You may trust that we will not be asked to visit. Meanwhile, in the year 2009 Wall Street bonuses increased 17% to 20.3 Billion dollars out of 55 Billion in profits, a 3-fold increase over the previous year (<u>Fox</u> <u>News</u>, quoting NY state's controller Tom Danapoli, Febryary 23, 2010).

Here's another example about how things are <u>still getting worse</u>: Some riper pumpkins! Most will now acknowledge that Fannie Mae and Freddie Mac were corruptly run by its officers for uncounted years; since they were quasi-governmental, <u>on purpose</u>, they were outside of normal legal structures. Thus, their leaders were able to exploit that "quasi" status for their own intemperate gain. Gretchen Margenson may write that "government inquiries found that between 1998 and 2004 senior executives at Fannie manipulated its results to hit earnings targets and generate $115 Million in bonus compensation." (<u>New</u> <u>York</u> <u>Times</u>, September 6, 2009; p.1 Sunday Business) All that is known and sadly understood. But, here's the corker, the icing on the cake or, by George, the real lining: These men and this woman, deceivers and connivers all, in the past year have had their attendant legal bills paid for by "we taxpayers (who) spent $2.43 Million to defend Mr. Paines, $1.35 Million for Mr. Howard, and $2.52 Million to defend Ms. Spencer." (p.6) In that same article, Alan Grayson, a Florida Democrat, correctly asks, "When did Uncle Same become Uncle Sap?" A long time ago, sports fans! God only groans.

A pattern emerges: We are continually closing the barn door after the pony has fled! Nearly always we fail to diagnose and predict a dangerous situation and we are, therefore, unable to employ small and corrective measures of mitigation or prevention. By this lax inattention we breed one catastrophe after another. I believe that America, like English in the late 30s, when she failed to recognize Hitler's growing threat," is lost in a passivist dream" (Said by the Winston Churchill character in the film, <u>A Gathering Storm</u>). We have become appallingly apathetic, asleep, dazed or indifferent to the nation's fate, self-absorbed by our own paltry and rutted drams, perhaps obsessed with the latest technological device which will not, as promised or supposed, lift us out of any doldrums. Thus, delays of justice abound, and, as William Shakespeare writes, "Defer no time. Delays have dangerous ends." (William Shakespeare. <u>King Henry VI</u>, Part I, Act III, Scene 2, line 33) Is it not time, now, finally, for us to listen to him?

I think we have been asleep for a very long time, perhaps, as my cousin, Jim Garvey, believes, from the time of John Kennedy's assassination: Since that critical and mournful day we have lost something. What? Our way; a talisman; the vision? A common path? Is it too dark to see? Dazed? Something ineffable. Perhaps the sense that we are all Americans and must be united. Do we care less for eachother? Are we not more splintered into always smaller groups? Can we no longer think as a team? Abuses are ignored, collusion flourishes, laziness is praised, chicanery increases, and all of this continues unabated. "How use doth breed a habit in a man," (William Shakespeare. <u>The Two Gentlemen of Verona</u>. Act V, scene 4, line 1); but is this habit of abuse and collusion and laziness and chicanery a good one for our nation? Can our nation long endure if these abuses are not deterred and thwarted? The old expression, "to fiddle while Rome burns," comes to mind. Too, the poet, Kenneth Patchen wrote a book of poems called, <u>Sleepers Awake</u>: Perhaps we should remember that verb from time to time. Or always, starting today.

We are in a crisis. We have the highest unemployment rate in 26 years, 9.7%, and that number is low by roughly half because it underreports those who work part-time and those who have given up trying to find work. If we are ever to end this self-made casino or mess we must think again of the forgotten man. Therefore, the president on vacation should <u>never</u> play golf with an investment banker, but, rather the little guy, say, the local owner of a tire shop which happens to be on the ropes financially. This is not a partisan issue, but a non-partisan one, asking the oldest question: What does it mean to be an American? What links me to my fellow man?

Again, we must think, with Franklin D. Roosevelt, of "the forgotten man at the bottom of the economic pyramid." (Radio Address April 7, 1932). He says, further: "We have always known that heedless self-interest was bad morals; we know now that it is bad economics." (SECOND Inaugural Address, January 20, 1937) In that single sentence is all that I have been trying to say with these scattered notes. From that same speech, FDR insists that we "need a change in the moral climate of America," and the same point must be broadly made today, but made with a greater gusto and strength and intensity since we have fallen so far, and therefore, have created a huge distance from solvency and safety and fairness, a gap which must be reduced. As Simon Johnson says there "needs to be a shift in power." [20] The financial oligarchy must be brought to an end, and the collusion at its core gotten rid of. Stern and steadfast reformers must <u>now</u>,

---

20 Simon Johnson Blog Conversations with Henry Blodget, April 21, 2009.

not later, act to enter the portals of power and eviscerate the corruption which abounds, cleaning house, becoming more than active, and dispensing with forever the idea that everyone can "dip one's beak" in the water as long as one does not get caught. To rob someone by picking his pockets is not the road we ought to be on.

We are all now, whether we like it or not, Lincolns after the disaster of Gettysburg on July 1 to July 3, 1863; we, too, no longer wonder what to say: We ask: Are we not in this together? Or, are some parts of our people more important? We must take the fiasco of 2008 and use it to transform this nation, achieving, as Lincoln writes, "a new birth of freedom." We must learn the lessons of 2008: That the banks self-interest shall <u>not</u> rule the land, and again discover a "government of the people, by the people, and for the people!" We must ask ourselves: what would Abraham Lincoln say confronted with this financial decadence? Wouldn't he say to Mary Shapiro or congress or the presented: Is this really the best you can do? He would roundly scold us just like he scolded his overly cautious general, always mustering troops, never fighting.

I bet he would say: One small and preferred class of people shall <u>not</u> have all the prerogatives and bounties of power. Again, we must think that we are all in this life together. We must abolish forever the foolish financial playpen that is now Wall Street. We must ponder anew what has happened to the older folks whose small IRA upon which they were to survive and depend on in their dotages, and which are now insignificant: How may we help them? Has anyone thought that this crash of 2008 has created millions of older people who will shortly, be out of scratch? We must readjust the pendulum so that financial institutions no longer possess unbridled power, nor operate under unfettered deregulation; and we must do these things sooner, rather than later, since, for every day that passes wherein these deleterious conditions persist, our nation, made of tender bounds which can be broken, weakens herself further and inexorably. Who shall master the puppet? Finally, we must think again, in a new and fresh way, that, still, we are united in a common goal, to live and to "breathe the same air" (JFK's American University speech of 1963, shortly before his death), that there is no segment of our society better than any other (for whom all sorts of privileges are to be metered), that we must be a people linked closely again with one another, not separated by access or power or networking connections, and that, without this greater and happy solidarity, we shall only founder the more. Many backward steps have been taken and they must be replaced. Self-interest must be dispensed with and replaced with the idea: What is best for all and not just a few special ones? Perhaps we must consider again with Shakespeare who reminds us of:

> "We few, we happy few, we band of brothers."
> William Shakespeare, <u>King</u> <u>Henry</u> <u>V</u>,
> Act IV, Scene 3, Line 60

Yet for now, shameful is our present path. Dissolute. Despicable. I am ashamed of how far we have gone down the wrong road; therefore, it is time to return to our roots of populism, equality, and fairness, all the famous words whose voices now grow faint; oh, to sing again, and gladly so. That shame will be chased away if we remember again FDR's forgotten man, the guy in the middle, the person being squeezed. The middle class has been getting itself pinched for decades. Who speaks for them? Nobody, or a few.

FDR got his idea about the forgotten man form William Graham Sumner (1840-1910), a political and social science professor at Yale, with whose apt words I close this discussion:

> "Wealth comes only from production, and all that the wrangling grabbers, loafers and jobbers get to deal with comes from somebody's toil and sacrifice. Who, then, is he who provides it all? The Forgotten Man... delving away in patient industry, supporting his family, paying his taxes, casting his vote, supporting the church and the school... but he is the only one for whom there is no provision in the great scramble and the big divide. Such is the Forgotten Man. He works, he votes, generally he prays - but he always pays."[21]

---

21 Sumner, The Forgotten Man (1883); a speech taken from Bartlett's Familiar Quotations; Little, Brown and Company, Boston; 1943; p. 876

Poor and content is rich, and rich enough.
> William Shakespeare, <u>Othello</u>, Act
> III, Scene 3, Line 185

O! What men dare do! What men may do! What men daily do, not knowing what they do!
> William Shakespeare, <u>Much</u> <u>Ado</u>
> <u>About</u> <u>Nothing</u>, Act IV, Scene 1, Line
> 18

A great pilot can sail even when his canvas is rent.
> Seneca (8 BC — 65 AD), <u>Epistles</u>,
> 30, line 3

When a true genius appears, you many know him my this sign: that all the dunces are in confederacy against him.
> Jonathan Swift, 1667-1745

I am not a child. I think for myself. No man can think for me.
> Chief Joseph, 1840-1904

Coda:
How to Fix the Gold Brick[22] Mess

Down the past several months, using a cautionary mind which, it is to be slimly hoped, has remained free of unnecessary entanglements (Thank you, General George Washington), I have written several party chairs, attorneys general, would-be representatives, seated senators and the like, saying to them that if they were to adopt some of these aforementioned, clearly populist stances: To rein in Wall Street, to help the little guy, not the Big Cheese, that immediately the majority of the people would be swayed and pleased enough to vote for that party in any next election.

In those letters I pledge with promises, promises, Jayne awash in the tub, her lovely, spankingly clean dirigibles ready for the kneading soap; yet, yes, I demean, I digress.) that I was neither didactic nor pleading, rather pragmatic: To wit, some samples of what I wrote to them:

---

22 An American phrase descriptive of any form of swindling (<u>Brewer's</u> <u>Dictionary</u> of <u>Phrase</u> and <u>Fable</u>, Revised Edition; by Ivor H. Evans; Cassell Publishers Ltd, London, 1988. P. 490)

1. How many of our financial institutions have garnered unrivaled power, a hellish transmutation that goes back many years and aims to harm the country we both love so much?

2. Many call out for greater regulation of Wall Street, yet the government has made it patently clear that it possesses neither the stomach nor the attention to detail required to do that job properly. The ruling class thus persists; and the <u>vox populi</u>, dismissed!

3. Indeed, Goldman Sachs is often derisively called Government Sachs since so often, and reversibly, its employees work for Uncle Sam. This unfortunate arrangement can only lead to many conflicts of interest — doing things for one's friends — that harm our country and its non-banker citizens. Nepotism: The word comes from the Italian word, il nepote, for nephew.

4. If the _____ Party, kind sir, were to say some of these admittedly controversial and populist things, it would alarm some bankers, yes, but more importantly coalesce the simmering wrath of so many average Americans who, through little fault of their own, have seen their finances squandered, quartered, lost.

5. What sort of nation have we become if the government feels the need to bail out beleagured banks (beleagured by dint of whose tainted hand?) which, then, in turn

and unconscionably, use those same proceeds to advance considerable, no, exorbitant, bonus monies to their own employees? Vile. Venal. Suctorial. Does no one every cry: "Foul!"?

6. And how do we as people, once these excesses are checked, restore our nation, rid ourselves of these mistakes, attempt judicious reforms, and establish anew the collective, not selective, good? "How" is always the most difficult question.

Were these notes to the powerful a faux pas? I think not; however, I have not heard back much in response but that silence is hardly surprising given the enormity of our country. I take no umbrage, since I write undercover and, anyway, am part of the hoi polloi or the great otig unwashed, a rustic having, thankfully, never gone to the schools of the Ivy League. Through those portals, those schools used to produce balanced thinkers who could attach a <u>wide</u> range of issues; now, nearly half (40%, as I wrote in the Preface) join the financial club, and are country suffers from that imbalance.

For purposes of kind discussion here I might mention another book on World War II: Hal Vaughan's book, <u>FDR's 12 Apostles: The Spies who Paved the Way for the Invasion of North Africa</u>. (The Lyons Press; Guilford, Connecticut, 2006). These 12 spies, young and risking all trying to make it a bit easier for the troops of Operation Torch, were mostly from the Ivy League, yes, Harvard, Yale, Princeton, etc.; and one must ask: If the call for that same service went out today to those same schools, what would be the response? Less, more, the same? The cynic in me says that the new Robert Murphy (their leader) would have to recruit from Montana State or Virginia Tech, but, like many times before, I, like Custer, could be wrong.

Next, I should like to propose, either for your pleasure or growing consternation, a series of concrete reforms that the government must soon enact and then police assiduously, that is, if it is serious about restoring some correct and harmonious equilibrium to our economic system.

1. Get rid of the national debt as much as possible. Don't fuel growth with debt. Pay as you go. With tiff, I note that our current president, joining so many others, has done the opposite, spending with prodigality, and, thereby, put our childrens' futures into ever greater distress. Gonzel.

2. We have to start making things again, and, yes, Hart, things like toasters. Not everyone can be in the finance, services or information industries! Rescind NAFTA immediately; it was a complete mistake from the get-go, as Jack may have said had we not prematurely handed him his hat.

3. The government ought to abolish hedge funds and derivatives since they are intrinsically destabilizing; also, any other, as-yet-unseen financial instruments similarly destabilizing must not be allowed by the pelfing grifters to be put in place. No more snow jobs.

4. Loans cannot be packaged and sold off to 3rd or 4th or 5th parties since, obviously, at some early juncture nobody knows what it is, exactly, that they own. This is common sense, Luckie.

5. Mortgage-backed securities, resolving credit arrangements, credit default swaps, and "risk"-

free arbitrage should be eliminated since they either are destabilizing or do not create real wealth. The snatch.

6. Programmed and block trading - as well as flash trading - must be gotten rid off, since they only benefit the "churning" institutional trader and harm the more traditional, long-term investor. Get rid of the gyp artist shenanigans, or else, I'll blow a fuse. No more oops, Nellie!

7. There are too many financial advisors and consultants: They should be avoided as carefully as one tries to avoid the plague or a muddle. They have little real investment, are vastly overpaid, and do not create real wealth. Copacetic? Ding how? I am really happy to read that Mr. Dick Field of the now-defunct Lehman, trying to launch a financial advisory firm, has had only modest results so far (<u>NY Post</u>; Mark DeCambre; 09/09/2009; p. 37) Good! Talk is cheap, tinpots!

I could say more, that, for example, banks should be prohibited from making donations to anyone in or out of government - no more currying favor, please, or that the revolving door whereby bankers take government jobs and vice versa must be jammed shut. But, I will stop there because the number seven is a lucky number, mine, and, especially, Mickey's, too. He had the number 6 for awhile but went into a slump, and, afterwards, when he came back up for the minors, he switched to 7. Everyone knows that it is a mystic or sacred number. There are seven deadly sins, seven hills of Rome, seven planets, seven sacraments and seven works of mercy. More to know but left unthought ; more to do but left unmade (<u>Brewers</u>, p. 106-108)

And that redeems me, Myrtle, of one other stay, to staunch or muster: Our congress, mostly, is a joke, the best that money can pay for. I hate like hell to say this (and to at last agree with my lovely wife, can you imagine, Ferguson, who before was told by his dotaging mind: You can't lodge here), but we must have term limits for Congress:

1. 4 terms for a House member equating, 4 x 2 = 8 years, and
2. 2 terms for a Senate member, equating to 2 x 6 = 12 years.

And after that, show them the door! Camels! Tailspin! Exit! Eye of the needle! If they stay too long, they take the money from lobbyists and become corrupted. Fatty pork: Rinds! Tripe! Offal! Simple. Soon, the lobbyists tell them what is to be in the bill. Simple. All independence is gone, and the place of Webster and Clay, Dirksen and Kennedy, is riddled with pork. Simple. If we have more turnover in Congress, we may see some small decrease in the corruption; yet, this is not something that can be guaranteed, so great is money's allure. Simple.

With the present situation, all things are suicidal. It, Congress, is like a perfectly fine plane, one steered steadfastly into the mountainside of San Jacinto, like what happened to Dino Martin, but, this time, it is on purpose.

I only call for this change draggingly. It is only because all attempts at campaign finance reform (real, not fake!) have, are, and will be curtailed, compromised, truncated or transmuted to born gossamer, torn to shreds in committee or, later, in court; in short, circumvented or got around as easily as a child of seven, I, so many tad years ago did, indeed, (here I tell the truth) steal loose candy from the candy store's open shelves. I am sorry. Pennies is no answer. Here, if you made a rule, a clever ratter will quick find a way 'round it. Too fast, too slow? Must be done, and no more teasers, Blanch...

The gentlemen who founded our country did not envision a Congressman who remains on the hill for many decades, surrounded by improvident lobbysits who turn his head with money, trips, girls, gifts, who knows what else. Talisker single malt Scotch, perhaps, will work for some, Gus. How far we have fallen! How far we have to climb back up out of the cesspool of our own making.

So, then, it is grim and getting grimmer. It seems that lobbyists' interests grow stronger daily, and not just those who work for bankers. Corruption of all sorts reigns.

To return to the above punchlist of simple and needed reforms, unless these provacative yet, return-to-the-basis pieces of advice are adopted, and adopted quickly, Wall Street will finish killing off its golden goose. So far, close to 2 years, few real reforms have been attempted and the hi-jinks continue. Let us recall again Nouriel Roubini's accurate remark: "Recovery will fail unless we break apart the financial oligarchy is blocking essential reform." He was absolutely right: Northing has happened and the banks are still in the catbird seat!

All lodgers: Let us step back a bit: What is the point of Wall Street? One thing: To earn a profit at least 2% higher than bonds; that is, say, to generate a 6% annual rate of return in a year when bonds produce at the 4% level. All of the 7 suggestions, and the others, are designed to return that some consistent profitability to the market. The playpen must be dismantled, now and step-by-step, and its deficiencies made transparent.

So, let me quote again from <u>Brewer's</u> regarding the golden eggs and the goose since, sometimes, it is the oldest tales that ring most true:

> "He grasped at what was more than his due and lost what was a regular source of supply. The Greek fable says a countryman had a goose that laid golden eggs; thinking to make himself rich, he killed the goose to get the whole stock of eggs at once, thus ending the supply."
>
> <u>Brewer's</u>; p. 496

Does this story not sound, unfortunately, accurate and familiar? It applies! Do we not tell these stories to our children (and ourselves!) anymore whereby we might learn something from them? Who can know this fable, and its moral, if he is never taught it? Alas, it is the story of 2008.

* * *

So, these men and women on the hunt or hustings, those who had the perogative and power and place to transmute the market for their own best result and all other causes be damned! And, if these be horses, they are renegade ones, frisky mustangs that must be corralled and if they be ships, they can be neither turned nor slowed, and are manned by all manner of complacent fools.

Of course, bankers will resist and mock all these invasive harangues. They like things just the way they are! They will act miffy, or condescend; they would scoff and belittle and jump down anyone's throat who so speaks. They will say that my changes are backward-looking, anti-capitalistic, and all the rest, words spoken by either a Neanderthal or an old, pappy guy or Luddite, someone whose wild and insolent inveiglements must be turned away or deterred.

Yet, I will say to them, with Will,

> " 'Tis not my speeches that you do mis-like, But 'tis my presence that doth troubles ye. Rancour will out."
>
> (William Shakespeare. <u>King Henry VI</u>, Part II, Act I, Scene 1, Line 138)

and, further, as if to placate or please:

> "I wear not
> My dagger in my mouth."
>
> (William Shakespeare. <u>Cymbeline</u>. Act IV; Scene 2; Line 78)

They will not wish much to converse or debate. And when they resist these claims and call them counterfeit, unlikely, or leftovers, as they will, we must say to them that all is changed, and changed utterly. Why! How? Proof: Lehman Brothers is gone, Bear Stearns is no more, Kidder Peabody is away! Is it right and fit to pretend that all is well? Any mind that has remained free, which is not too-tied-to the stepping need for profit, or any other dictum must say that fundamental reforms must begin; and the only questions ought to be:

1. Which ones, Shirley, and
2. When do we start, Charles?

It does the vet no good to say that the dog is not very sick.

So, come, let us gather friends around here, at my affable stocking table. I am not alone in saying these things, and not at a swords' point, either. The average American already knows that Wall Street is a toxic playpen, corrupt as Napoli or Tammany. We have risked Avernus and are there already, at the lake's edge in Campania which is the only gate to hell (<u>Brewer's</u>, p.64). For example, Dr. Nouriel Roubini, Professor of Economic at New York University's Stern School of Business concurs saying that "the American capitalist financial system has collapsed and cannot be revived in its current state."[23] I do not know if he were to agree with me that 2008's meltdown, in which many, many families lost 75% of their net worth, was the result not of an international subtertuge, but, was one, rather, created by we Americans ourselves, from within, engendered by our own excessive and vacuous pride (or, to use Mr. Cohan's word again: Hubris) whereby financial leaders, goaded by their own over-reaching egos, <u>simultaneously</u> made a <u>series</u> of false assumptions, just like Custer did.

To wit:

1. Markets will not crash.
2. Markets are never irrational.
3. Excessive debt levels may be managed.
4. The USA alone controls its destiny.
5. The boom time will last.
6. Corrective measures will work and quickly so.
7. The bigger the bank, the more stable it is.

Point number seven, that a bigger bank is more stable (or a bigger company becomes too important to be dissolved) reflects the collusion at the oligarchy which is at the heart of the issue, the hub or nexus of this financial disease from which all symptoms appear. John Carlson, the Seattle - booed conservative talk show host, presciently writes:

---

23 April 4, 2009 at <u>Huffington</u> <u>Post.</u>

> It is time we change the paradigm from "too big to be allowed to fail" to "too big to be allowed."

I ask AGAIN: Why weren't federal anti-trust laws enforced? Why are they <u>still</u> <u>not</u> generally enforced? Answer: There is considerable, wide-ranging and nefarious collusion at the oligarchy, and like any particularly nasty disease (whether large like tuberculosis which killed my mother, or small like athlete's foot which bothered my father) it can be very hard to get rid of.

Who wants to do the job of new and rigorous regulation? What titan? What Vulcan or Zeus? It is, or would be, were the job to be broached, a clearly thankless one, and all involved would have to have the hide of a rhino or cape buffalo, nerves of steel, sinews as cable, and with the gloves off (admitting, yoemen, all the cliches at once, including glove money, a bribe or worse, <u>Brewer's</u> p.486) and still, the fight may be one lost.

This person, this knight or warlord, would have to have the steely character of George Washington who, nearing the end of his 2nd term in 1797, was approached by many citizens to stay on for a third. He wanted to farm at Mount Vernon, but, more crucially, he understood that the nation continually needs <u>new</u>, <u>fresh</u>, <u>untainted</u> leaders, the better to eschew corruption. And, besides, we had not fought the long and difficult war with England (1775-1783) so that we could replace one king, George III, with another: Himself. Power is best exercised if it be temporary.

Meanwhile, waggers, the hubris continues. Business leaders still do not believe that they have done much wrong, or that they have been beaten with their own, self-pointed weapons. Wounded by shrapnel, tied up in knots? No: Still, they deny culpability of the smallest measure. I believe the pertinent phrase is: To be hoisted with his own petaral.

Involved in the danger intended for others, one is caught in one's own trap (<u>Brewer's</u>, p. 853). In <u>Hamlet</u>, Shakespeare writes,

> Let it work;
> For 'tis sport, to have the engineer
> Hoist with his own petard; and it shall go hard
> But I will delve one yard below their mines,
> And blow them at the moon.

> William Shakespeare. <u>Hamlet</u>. Act
> III, Scene 4; Line 212

To speak more centrally, at base, what lead to this mess? Answer: Too many people said to themselves: "My knowledge is complete, and my areas of expertise have no limit." (My reading tells me that the last person who could make that claim with validity was Erasmus, the Dutch Theologian (1466?-1536). He possessed all the then-knowledge of the known world, before <u>both</u> expanded). Obviously, it was an overweening ego that inspired much of the meltdown, a voice inside one's head urging caution against caution, saying, "I can control things," and most perversely preaching that "If I am happy, the world is happy." Therefore, the elderly woman who just lost most of her IRA may be disregarded; therefore, the family (ours) that just saw its net worth go from 4x or 5x to 1x, does not need to be apologized to; and, for that reason fantastical bonus checks, fed by taxpayers' monies and even though many firms showed horrific write-down losses in '08, may still be written. The peak of haughtiness!

By definition, the arrogant man does not think himself arrogant, just as the adulterer does not share grief with an unrequited wife, or the bank robber does not recognize his sin against the hapless depositors. All think that they are plainly entitled. And many peoples' arrogance may go unchecked, especially if one's life is not stained by tragedy or war, if the boom times seem limitless, or if anxiety or a child's sickness do not ever come to call. Then, there will be no soft whisper in the ear to say, "My knowledge is incomplete, or, dreaming again my old dream, thinking with the Greeks that "All Glory Passes." (Thank you to the maestro, Mr. Coppola, who inserted those words as the last ones in the screenplay that he wrote for the trenchant film, Patton). A prideful man, pitching forward with perhaps more testosterone than would be favorable, is the one more likely to take risks, even with other people's money which he shortly before had been charged to guard. Thus, Will writes:

> He that is proud eats up himself;
> Pride is his own glass, his own trumpet,
> His own chronicle.
>
> William Shakespeare. Troilus and
> Cressida. Act II, Scene 3, Line 153

He does not allow himself to think "I may be wrong." He unhoards reserve and admonishes against restraint. And, if caught in a calamity caused by his own unwise counsel, he will be loath to admit the mistake or to allow for even a tincture of an apology. Yet, this is not logical, since, are we not all imperfect beings, fully capable of errors in judgement or deed, to the rate of, at least, seeds of one a day (like the apple, Chapman, like the apple!)?

It is not surprising, then, that this slim volume will, near its end, (thanks be to Minerva) turn on this most fundamental of questions, that is, to what extent a man should be humble. Sophocles advises:

> Do not persist, then, to retain at least
> One sole idea, that the thing is right,
> Which you mouth utters, and nought else beside.

Sophocles. <u>Antigone.</u>

These thoughts are not new, nor the issues that they then raise close to a solution final.

* * *

To regear the axle, to refocus the telescope closer for a few more spee moments. For us, the time of trouble approached and thus, the more quickly so, as if we were manning the smallest <u>barchetta</u> <u>verde</u> on the most swollen or Solent of seas, churning, turgid, and we were met by swamping, massive tidal waves of financial stormy blue-grey discord which wanted to sink our small ship anxiety arrived. During those perilous days of not so long ago, surrounded by debt, circled by creditors, unable to pay even the tiniest bill, I recalled the short story of Stephen Crone, "The Open Boat," and its theme of the world's indifference to those that struggle against Nature.

Yet, I was soon wrong for, within days, through the aid of kind friends and relatives (more friends than relatives, that is to be sure, but that thought makes for another and meaner story, and not this one), we scrapped by. Often, whenever we were truely up against it (down on one's uppers), something very good happened: For example, we sold a truck for decent money, or a few sticks of furniture. Too, as a family, we began to pray together, asking for help, saying:

"What, then, must we do?"

Luke 3:10

or,

"How to engender strength, My Lord? It cannot come from Me since I am weak and my thoughts

are paltry. I will no longer Search my insignificant
brain, but Yours.

Scores of times our pleading prayers were answered (and
then we thanked God since it is good, while praying, to
not <u>always</u> ask). Always we followed Winston Churchill's
dictum to "Keep Buggering On." (KBO) That word, to
bugger, means something else again in England, but 'tis
another country, and, besides the wench is dead, but, does
she have a sister? My Marlsive is not amused.

Occasionally with time, the vitriol mildly diminishing,
I would think back upon what the Italians call, "i uomini
tangenti" or the moneyed men who have gone off-track.
Doing so, I came up with a few further conclusions:

1. The bonlser have a bad business model; they
    seem to care more about themselves than their
    customers who are only a means to their end:
    Profit. Sooner or later, most customers do not
    like to be treated poorly. Charging fees after
    no equity appreciation? No. Eventually, since
    it is not a two-way street, rather 'heads I win,
    tails you lose,' they will have fewer customers
    to bank to. Good. Nicolo does not win <u>all</u> the
    fights.

2. We went to them because one cannot know
    everything (thank you, my friend, James
    Hunnicut); that is, ours was a fiduciary
    relationship and we trusted that they would
    make money and guard our trust. They
    performed poorly, not anticipating much of
    anything. Their advice was neither clear nor
    accurate. They still feel, apparently, little
    responsibility for poor performance. Morals? It

is hard to shame the shameless. They wash their hands and move on.

3. Wall Street needs, now, a headstrong and independent leader, the "benign despot" of Plato's <u>Republic</u>, a damning and irascible king, one supreme commander for all the forces, someone strong and virtuous who will maintain order, fairness and the sanctity of society. <u>He must look out for the Little Guy first</u>! He will prevent any new erosions into further, dark chaos. The concept is: To matter, to court. Yet, for now, conflicting boundary disputes deflect any coordinated effort. And for that reason, most bankers are pleased.

4. Arrogance abounds, uncontained, unrestrained. "For professing themselves to be wise, they become fools." (Romans 1:22.) They thought, with God, that they knew what would happen tomorrow! A jumbo joke! The waste of paper in sending out all those rosey predictions, all of which turned out to be bunk.

And so, happily, mostly, we left them and what they may or may not have said behind. It does little good to look backwards (Satchel Paige, the stupendous and surprising pitcher: No one, 'cept his mama, knew his real age!). We resolved to look forward, and to be unfloppable. We must model ourselves on Raymond Asquith, son of the Prime Minister, mercilessly killed in the first world war and whom Churchill described as "cool, poised, resolute, matter-of-fact debonair. [24]

---

24 Jack Kennedy: <u>The Education of a Statesman</u>. Barbara Leaming W.W. Norton, NY 2006 p.57

And so, impassively, we survived, just. Once, cleaning up in our garage, I would glance up at a large framed photograph by O. Winston Fink entitled "sometimes the Electricity Fails," (August 8, 1956). It shows young (soon to be petting?) couple in what might be a convertible Pontiac Chieftain, and an older man is trying to fill up their tank with gas. It is a warm summer night, and a large freight train looms in the background, but the pump, the tall, old-fashioned kind with the small bubble in the clear glass cylinder on top, the pump will not work: Sometimes the electricity fails. Sometimes things do not work out the way that we had planned. "Oft expectation fails, and most oft there where most it promises." (William Shakespeare. <u>All's Well That Ends Well</u>; Act II; Scene 1; Line 144.) Or, one might say from the same play: "I am a man whom fortune both cruelly scratched." (Act IV, Scene 2, Line 27)

In the face of those circumstances, one can either give in to lassitude or else become more determined and more stoical. That is to say, gathering the latter: Of course, things did not work out so well.! Of course, the electricity sometimes fails! What else would you expect, Ethel? Of course, you got a bum steer! Of course, we are on the ropes, but we must face facts!

Then, to survive and endure (we will leave the discussion of whom or what prevails for another day's nostrum, William), one must become more indifferent, expecting far less, appreciating more, adopting impassivity to both pain or pleasure. Then, "passions and appetites should be rigidly subdued", (<u>Brewer's</u>, p. 1072) In truth, there is no other choice, else melancholy enters the room for a long checkmate's stay.

Clearly, the so-called boom years are over; this is a not-unhappy circumstance wherein our country might be kindly changed for the better with a greater frugality, lowered expectations, fewer private planes, and all the unnecessary other extravagances. Who said, "Less is more?" Or, "It is fun to be frugal!" What is the loss if we drive smaller cars (Still, and quickly: Toujours la vitesse!), buy plums only from our continent, or take vacations closer to home? Perhaps, the meltdown of '08 will truly help America and Americans, bringing us closer together, curtailing the boom years' self-interest a tad or mitra, linking us a bit more closely together. Was it not the composer and lyricist Irving Berlin who wrote "Life can be as simple as a nursery rhythm?" ("All of My Life"). Perhaps, too, fewer people will go around, mouthy, a gob open, saying, "If I am happy, the world is happy." Mither and papa would say to me that that would be a good thing, and they look down now from on high.

Besides, maybe that upper class club one I do not wish to join anyway; maybe its dues are too damned expensive; maybe I do not wish to pay all those friggin' bills which grow faster than my equity's return; perhaps if I join that club I will inevitably become the archetypal snotty rich bastard (one word or two?). Not something said as a choice, but with the realization that, if one has a bit of money, the leeches come to attach upon one's leg, stealing or secreting away all the vital fluids. Who want to pay thousands a year in property taxes, house insurance, and the like? We now have a two-tier salary system in the USA with the poor vastly overshadowed by the very rich: Pro athletes, drug dealers and, yes!, financial types who are mostly overpaid. The middle class is getting squeezed inordinately by all sorts of spiraling costs. My father, who all the time complained about nearly everything, never uttered a word of resentment about our house insurance; that is because, then, it was negligible! Oh, how times have changed! Thus, the inviting motorhome, here I come!

Then, we join the near pauper's club. We eat beans and take away our own trash. We hire out for little. People drive my our splendid, heavily encumbered home, and, seeing me at some mundane chose, ask if I am the caretaker. Not wishing to lie, yet not trying to disappoint, I say, "Yes," but leave out the salient fact that my wife and I are, also, the owners. I think about how the roles and expectations between the tenant and the lord, the poor and the rich, often become confused or, indeed, switch. As an owner I no longer wish to hire out a job to a local who will probably change far too much, inflate his time, and perform the task poorly. So, as a grunt or old stick, I will grab a shovel (what my stock used to call "an Irish fan or spoon") as quick as Glauber Salts will purge the bowels (Brewer's, p. 484).

Now, we look ahead and long regret little. Our expectations have lowered and our perenncial wants are less. We tend to associate with the average folks and not so much with the cotton sweater crowd, it draped nonchalantly, yet decorously, around their slender necks. As Shakespeare says "My friends were poor, but honest." (All's Well That Ends Well; Act I; Scene 3, Line 192). We began to eat soup by the gallon, that is, soup made by soaking the bean in water overnight like people used to do before soup could be bought in cans. Too, we started to eat all manner of cheaper vegetables, like kale and cabbage, turnips and swedes, like all the other impoverished ones before us.

One further glad result is that we are no longer put off, or scunnered by the feeble and empty pronouncements of money managers. Glad day: We no longer have to speak to them! Hooray! No more slinging the bull! We no longer have to listen to their hollow predictions, ambiguous advice, weak excuses, or lame justifications for pitiful performance, see fees collected yet not earned, or watch their proven inability to predict or foretell anything! In particular, I no longer have to listen to their excessive use of the conditional tense: the Market <u>could</u> rise, etc., and that in itself is a happy and considerable blessing. Of course, the Market could rise, and, at the same time, pigs could fly! But not today, not today.

Too, one may speak, or use some fuller language. With this book, I no longer have to ask the money boys if I may speak. Their condescension is nowhere about. A glad thing. A captain's blessing. I say to them: May I speak? May I? Again: To have ceded so much power to a group so insular, so proudly entrenched within layered realms of unchallengeable power was a mistake: We should have told them to go to hell all the time, that is, <u>every time they made a mistake</u> — which was nearly all the time. At least, fickle mobbers, they will no longer play the old gooseberry with us. That is our new rue, or "herb of grace," something handed down to our family by a gracious God who sees all and does not mock our mistakes with derision or immodest catcalls.

Finally, (and here is where we all are slave mamelukes (<u>Brewer's</u>, p. 705 united in huffy dedication against those who purport to know so much), I will never again trust these feeblers, indolents, those rash speculators <u>who may never lose</u>, those tart meanderers from Thule, greenhorners or Tom Noddys all: To the fore — I will never again trust these uncagey fellows to tell me even the time; and many others will join me to do the untame same. They do not know that their fancy halcyon days are done.

Too, one may predict that the country, after this butchered hackery or Hara-Kiri, will be slightly less of a sissy nation . (Read book of the same title by John Strausbaugh and "<u>How America Became a Culture of Wimps and Stoopits</u>" (Virgin Books; New York, 2007). Maybe there will be a healthy shift away from the so-called financial industry, those whose pants never get dirty, whose hands never become calloused, where leaders make far too much money for far too little real work, towards vital production, the source of true wealth. Maybe the schemers and skimmers, the lotuseaters, the churners and the dervish, the jackals and toadies, will repent their vile, monetary reaches which do not enrich this nation but decay it, in kind favor making a new mechanism to forge a more lasting and true prosperity, one shared and not a dangerous Matterhorn from which one may fall. Maybe that 40%, the high percentage of graduates from the Ivy League that go into Wall Street (so Gargantuan the starting salaries, so Herculean that first Christmas bonus!), maybe that number will thankfully decline, riffling, by some small measure, so that some men will chose the elusive profit somewhere else, as in making shirts, like Hathaway, or producing wire cables like we used to do back before the St. Louis Browns moved to Baltimore and became the Orioles, that is, in 1954, when I was three and just starting to pee on my own: Sorry. I become cantankerous after time. Withershins, she, we, may go in the opposite directions away from the gammon to save herself, our country and her hostage people, then held, and still transfixed by too much gold and unranking of will. We are still at war with ourselves. Blinded, we were, like the one-eyed man in the shirt ad: Not to see. If we are wise enough to wish to see again, first, someone needs to turn on the light, as Goethe said on his deathbed: "More light! Mehr licht!"

'Tis a bit more ligan, fellow sailors, or disparate items still attached to the boot. (<u>Brewer's</u>, p. 668) your patience, please.

Pope Benedict XVI recently completed an encyclical entitled <u>Charity</u> in <u>Truth</u>, or <u>Caritas</u> in <u>Veritate</u>. He writes about proportionate profit and the uses of profit, the windows of fairness that must exist between vendors and clients, and

how an unspoken social contract exists in the marketplace
whether it is recognized or not. He writes:

> "We are still at war with ourselves. Without truth,
> without trust and love for what is true, there is
> no social conscience and responsibility, and social
> action ends up serving private interests and the logic
> of power."
>
> Ignatius Press, Fort. Collins, Colorado

The question obviously becomes: Where have Christian
Business Ethics gone? Out the window with a rake-hell's
progress? Is it morally correct for the leaders of these
banks, many of them actually losing money, to garner such
stupendous bonuses and salaries when nearly 20% of the
work force is either unemployed, or, in the new, equally
sad fashion, underemployed, examples of the part-timing
of America.

Let us turn again to the Pope. He writes:

> "Once profit becomes the exclusive goal, if it is
> produced by improper means and without the
> common good as its ultimate goal, it risks destroying
> wealth and creating poverty."
>
> Pope Benedict XVI, <u>Caritas</u> <u>in</u>
> <u>Veritate</u>; Ignatius Press; p. 21

I wonder how many of today's rajah-bankers (Such kings!
Such pedagogues!) would not heartily scoff at the Pope's
cautionary words. And, I know that there exists a huge and
growing gap between the Pope's gentle ethos and the thievery
and free-for-all recklessness of the street. How to close it when
the bankers admit to little wrong and refuse to apologize, as
ours have done? For, all that has happened in the years after
the 2008 collapse is this: Financial leaders have resisted most

reforms and federal regulators have argued over the perimeters of power. Someone with some guts needs to enter the Ganelon fray of black-hearted treachery (<u>Brewer's</u>, p. 466); we need someone who is not from the club and who does not wish to be liked. He must ask: "Why have the federal anti-trust laws not been enforced for decades?" He must be very thick-skinned. He must be absolutely unbreakable and untouchable. He must not play golf, Mr. President, with anyone whom he intends to monitor. He must be a bulldog and virtuous and unrelenting if this mess, this fiasco and catastrophe crafted by our own dirty hands, (as if on purpose, so dedicatedly was the House of Cards made (re: Mr. Cohen)), is ever to be put behind us. All possible efforts must be carried out to make Wall Street safe again for the average investor. The question is: Are we still a nation?

Pronto, the pendulum must swing back to normalcy so that the ruling class of economic royalists is dissolved. Engendered brick by brick by collusion at the oligarchy, this shabby house of decadence must be deconstructed, taken apart, again, brick by brick. So far, inertia rules; and one must ask: Is this the best that we can do? Pitiful. Pis-aller. Malebolge. Worst course. Iniquity in that order. (<u>Brewer's</u>, p. 869,703).

* * *

Halfway through the composition of this small exercise, I stumbled upon (Inadvertently or on purpose, the mind guided by God or divining its own ends in a mysterious way?) Tom Brokaw's book <u>The</u> <u>Greatest</u> <u>Generation</u>. Back in 1998, just after it was released, I had givien it to my father, who was then chronically ill and had much time to read.

The book mirrors his own life: He, too, like so many others in the book, had survived the Depression and World

War II. So much of life was difficult! During the war when my dad, a lieutenant, served as a navigator on transport ships mostly in the South Pacific and Indian Oceans, two horrendous things happened to my parents: Their first daughter, Nanette, a child actress with an Irish face and black curly hair, died of Leukemia in 1943, and their second girl, Patricia Kay, was born the same year with Down's Syndrome. My father did not know of either sorrowful event for months, so poor was the military's communication then. How deeply my mother must have suffered! Eventually, they got through it, but it was not easy. Four more children arrived over time, and life went on. Through it all, they relied on God and each other for help and direction.

Coming out of the war, as Brokaw writes, my parents like so many others, were quite stoical, they knew how to "knuckle under," to get things done, and they were never disheartened by difficulties. They always felt that they could get through the war, that they could survive. They believed that God would help them, but they had to ask Him. When I was a child, if they saw a family in our neighborhood who needed help, theirs was a "selfless response." (Brokaw, p. 388) They took great pride in national service, and when the Vietnam debacle occurred in the late 60's, they regretted the diviseness that that war engendered. More than anything, they believed in the concept of the common welfare. As Brokaw concludes:

> "Most of all, there is the need to reinstate the concept of common welfare in America, so that the nation doesn't squander the legacy of this remarkable generation by becoming a collection of well-defined, narrowly cast special interest fiefdoms, each concerned only with its own place in the mosaic. (P. 388-389)

167

Doesn't that sound like what the banks have been up to?

Instead, we must again be a united, not divided nation. In corralling the banks, bringing those high desert mustangs back to the barn, we must speak with one voice. We must fight for what we believe in (as our parents did against Hitler and Japan), saying simply that the world that the banks would have is not just. And, as Senator Daniel Inouye says in the book,

"The one time the nation got together was World War II.

We stood as one. We spoke as one. We clenched our fists as one." (P. 349)

My parents understood that we all stand together. After the war, my father gave financial advice to hundreds of widows and my mother advised pregnant teens and abused women. They never thought only of themselves.

As we retrench, I think that the only way that national unity may return is to bring back the idea of national service: Everyone of able mind and body at age eighteen serves two years for his or her country. This would instill in all a greater feeling of country, of belonging, of patriotism, and of helping the other person. Unless we try something like this soon, the selfishness, which sparked the banks long slide towards greed and excess, will only continue to the detriment of all.

* * *

Last thoughts:

Playing basketball poorly in high schools decades ago I slowly learned that if someone on the other team pushed me around roughly, a bit too boisterously, like a rustic might under the boards, he became my mentor and I returned the coarse favor, just so, maybe elevating the physicality just a tiddling notch, judiciously, to tell him that I am not someone who can be pushed around. To defend onself. To compel respect. To be "Fierce in enmity to all who crossed him." (Joyce Carol Oates. <u>Blonde</u>. Fourth Estate, London, 2000. P. 688; speaking of, by the way, President Kennedy)

* * *

I recall the old Navy slogan: "Don't tread on me!" Who knows all flags? Watch yourself, pogue! Are you a sissy? Where's the old man? Do you have a mama, a one-and-only?

Careful: All passing ships can be predatory. Floating coffins. I wish I'd never met them but can't go backwards. Turn the T.S. page, Satch. Stai attento! Be gremlin alert! Just like family: Predacious (and that doesn't mean pretty flowers). You can't know SNAFU everything so you have to trust that they know what the devil they're doing. No scuttlebutt. Ribbon happy. Pull rank. Praise the Lord, TNT, and pass the ammunition. I just did, lunkhead. It's because I'm all browned off. Look, you coffee cooler, I need some rack time. Make do. Understand tiger? Or are you low on amps and voltage? Or, at least so asks Mr. David Shulman, (Born 1912, Died when?) Who retides me, as well, that Loose Lips Sink Ships. (Dickson, Paul. <u>War</u> <u>Slang</u>. Brisol Park Book, New York, NY, 1994). Who can recall all the World War II war slang. Chop chop; answer me, you ronchie eaglet, or has Cupid's itch put you over the blue wall?

Perhaps I ought to explain more deeply the above military riff. What is its place here? It is simply, safely to say: We cannot know all, none of us, not even the preordained bankers. The world is a large and complicated place. Who among us knows that a knuckle buster is a crescent wrench, Mexcian strawberries are beans, or that a fart sack is a bedroll? Who knows that Bolivia once had a coastline? (Or was it Paraguay?) <u>Brewer's</u> says the same! We are headed towards the Heisenberg's Uncertainty Principle whereby as soon as something is fixed, it moves, and is, thus, the more unknowable. Therefore, intelligence has its limits in a constantly changing world: As soon as a fact is seen and declared, it shifts and must be redetermined, redefined. Yet, the bankers, puffed up with pride, high-brows, arrogant as some full bird colonels, thought that they could predict the future, and that the market was stable. Ha! Fugazi! They were wrong , but most have not yet said so. Probably, the same habit of mind: Everything is OK because I say so and know the world; my knowledge persists and will continue to pertain.

* * *

Doing nothing is treasonous, and dawdling along spells doom for our country:

> "Great Caesar fell.
> O! What a fall was there, my countrymen;
> Then I, and you, and all of us fell down,
> Whilst bloody treason flourished over us."
>> William Shakespeare. <u>Julius</u> <u>Cesear</u>.
>> Act III, Scene 2, Line 191

I am ashamed of ourselves, still sleeping. Karl Popper asks,

> "What is one to do when the <u>demos</u>, the people, freely decides to resign its power to a despot?"

That is what we have done: Given up our authority to the craven. As A. D. Nattal says in <u>Shakespeare</u>: <u>The</u> <u>Thinker</u>:

"Democracy can do many things. It can even commit suicide."

(P. 173)

* * *

May I speak, or should I monitor more carefully my utterances, metering them ashamedly, using, perhaps, Eliot's "coffee spoons"? Chop-chop! Hurry? 37? Luke! What's your answer, Mister Deadhead?

* * *

In their brazened ability to tell both the goat and the sheep what to do, they declared themselves a ruling class. They took on the role of Empire Purple, a king's color obtained form costly shellfish (<u>Brewer's</u>. P.906). They are a group entitled and bejeweled, conjuring statues and elevated rank, using condescension, derision and impertinence as various weapons. Each member is clever, cagey, adroit, disinclined to show his hand. All would be good at poker or chess. Hussars. Asleep at the switch. Thistles, the Scottish symbol of defense. Grab your hat, boys: It's time for this peashooter to peel off.

* * *

Perfidy: Deliberate breach of faith, calculated violation of trust, treachery.

Though the word has become strangely out of fashion, the bad character it describes is ever popular, yet its usage is not popular among the sharks.

* * *

We have been absolute fools and it is time to take back our country from those for whom self-interest is all.

We have, also, to return to those square, old-fashioned values that say "I will not take that check unless I have earned it."

We have, here, finally, a story, like all others, about how, after some sort of disaster, death, catastrophe or grief, one learns to go on.

* * *

This will never do: There guys don't know that their day in the sun is already over. Blind as bats, they are like so many who have dallied too long at this bar, and who are now clueless, out to lunch. People in general understand to the core that the bankers have gone too far, and that, therefore, they, the scalpers and whelps, need to eat copious crow. It all depends on what sort of country one expects to have. What do we dream for? That is what we shall receive. A higher level of honor? Shame on whom? The definition of average? Speaking clearly, what words may ever reach you?

In any case: Here's the deal. Sooner or later, you have to slay the Giant, the Cyclops, the g.d. gorilla. Got it? Jackson, are you paying attention to me, yet, or what? Fiddlesticks.

* * *

Like Babe Ruth, I don't like people telling me what to do. Most Americans feel the same way (about the banks). Time to rouse, awaken, kick up a fuss, to stop the dilly-dally and fix this country. NOW.

* * *

This sort of thing, preeminent corruption at the core, has happened many times before. I remember back to the early years of the 20th century in Los Angeles. The big shots wanted the City of Angels to expand exponentially (at that time it was smaller than Pasadena); yet, it lacked that all-important element: Water. There was only enough indigenous water for 250,000 people. So, what to do? Why, steal it, of course. So they did!

Engineer William Mulholland, under the auspices of L.A.'s Department of Water and Power, traveled 250 miles northward to the eastern side of the Sierra Nevada mountains and there he found the massive Owens Lake. He knew, too, that because of the slight, but constant, slope upwards from Los Angeles that once he got the water flowing in pipes or ditches that it would flow easily a la Sigmore Venturi; southward, downhill through the Tehachapi Mountains all the way to L.A.

So, they stole it, the water, right under the complicit eyes of the law. Once again, all tadpoles and newts, collusion at the oligarchy triumphed. Overnight, or close to it, it emerged. Ranchers were put out of business, and the environment radically harmed; but the important business deal was accomplished: The big shots in L.A. would have the water necessary so that real estate speculation, that fractured bedrock upon which California's economy has been foolishly based for 100 greasy years, might commence. Within a few years the flourishing agriculture of the San Fernando Valley was replaced by thousands of tract homes, but, what the heck, many fortunes had been made.

Still, many of the ranchers up north were angry. So, they sabotaged the aqueduct carrying the water, continually bombing it and blasting it apart, much to the growing consternation of the Department of Water and Power. To mitigate, the DWP decided to put a series of smaller reservoirs much closer to L.A., in fact, ringing it, the better to keep watch over them, protecting them from the pissed off ranchers. The DWP put pressure on Mulholland to build one of them above Piru on the Santa Clara River in Ventura Country just north of L.A. Mulholland did not care for the site because of the loose, friable soil, but because of that pressure, <u>which</u> <u>he</u> <u>was</u> <u>too</u> <u>weak</u> <u>to</u> <u>resist</u>, he built it anyway. One November night, after the dam was just built, a violent rainstorm hit the Santa Clara Valley. The reservoir was filling too quickly, too quickly! Soon, it developed a small leak, and, then, suddenly, it gave way; it was three minutes before midnight, March 12, 1928. The collapse killed 200 people at the base of the dam and 200 Indians who had been living at the mouth of the Santa Clara River where it washes into the Pacific Ocean between Ventura and Oxnard. (They took many of the bodies to the gym at Santa Paula High School for examination; I played much poor, error-filled basketball there in the 60's.) This disaster is one of the largest ever, but it is mostly unknown. The dam was named after the patron saint of animals and Italy, and our family now has, nearly, his distemper, St. Francis's, that is, the condition of being moneyless, or impecuniosity. (<u>Brewer's</u>, p. 453)

Then, things did not bode well for Mulholland. He felt a never-ending guilt for his complacent hand in building the ill-fated dam in that poor location. He never forgave himself for his part in killing all those people, and he died a broken and dispirited man.

But, one day before that, at a DWP ceremony marking the new release of Owens Lake water from one of the city's reservoirs, he said, bitterly to the crowd, sensing his own complicity in the scheme "There it is - Take it!"

In a similar fashion, the many dull denizers of the Fed and the SEC and all the other groups that are meant to regulate, to control, to corral Wall Street, they, the corrupt, compromised, and lazy, can turn to the happy, snide smiling leaders of the banks (who now have <u>more</u> than what they wanted) and say the same, "Here's your Wall Street: There it is - Take it!"

And that reminds me, too, of another, more salty tale: In Federico Fellini's movie, "Amarcord" (I remember, in dialect), the very attractive, slightly older woman, who pines for love and never finds it (until the very end when another man in uniform snags her), she is named, leeringly, with tongue-in-cheek, to see if we will get the joke, "Gradisca", meaning, "Help Yourself." The things some people say... Ma, non peccato. This time, now, I see that it is snowing hard outside so I am going home. Much of the material for this segment on Los Angeles comes from Margaret Leslie Davis' book, <u>Rivers in the Desert</u>: <u>William Mulholland and the Inventing of Los Angeles</u>. Harper Collins, NY, 1993. Comeuppance. California: Real Estate. 'Tis another's tale.

* * *

At this point, tanglefoots, we would all be smart (perspicacious, prudent, Palladian, principled, procedural, proportional, pigeoned and, therefore, pepped out, using as many "p" words as there are pennies to count some jack) to ask, to task ourselves with one simple quotient question:

"Do we wish the USA to still be the central economic and therefore, political force in the world? Yes, or no, Ned, and I'll give you 20, flat broke minutes to respond."

Members of Brokaw's Greatest Generation would answer that question, "Yes!" in less than 20 seconds; but, many of them are slipping away, under the kingfisher waters, so that their tale of patriotism and zeal and common welfare and simple pride: That we are a decent people who will do the right thing, is one not so 'oft told. Twice told once, but now, the less so. Hence, times change and new, fiercer models emerge. Many would say, No, that we have ruled too hard for too long and that since Vietnam, our influence has been primarily nefarious or hokum. The question is not a hard one, a real brain teaser or a mind twister that will drive you nuts, bonko, but something that must be asked or tasked to all, of us since it has to do with the money, pelf, the green stuff, jack or ookus, as has this book, yarn, or spiel. This country: What she dreams for, she shall receive.

It seems to me worrying, grousing, grauming, as one does, that we may have all of this grabby, greedy, snookering going on, but done on purpose, to make all the countries equal, so that no one governor may have any more favor or power than any other, not like when I was born in Truman's term when we, benevolently, benignly ruled the world. With caution. Now, our debt grows like the addiction of a hopped up, gowed heroin user, and, now, should India or China wish to make a margin call on that monstrous loan, we would be as broke as bankrupt in an afternoon: The grand bounce. All would be lost! All! In selling away Wall Street, in giving it away to the investment banks as a token of corruption, collusion, greed or not being able to see this Asiatic future, are we not badgering ourselves, giving ourselves a cancer of the most pernicious sort (pancreatic, Tom Long?), something from which we might never recover.

We have knocked ourselves on our own asses, so you have to wonder if it is on purpose, so that all countries might be equal.

The people who believe that wampum theory do not think the United States is at all that special; they do not think that it is pleasantly ordained by God to have a more powerful and friendly role in world. Some do not think we can be, after Vietnam, a force for good in the world. Some of them do not believe in capitalism at all, whether properly controlled or not, and are merely apathetic at Wall Street's malarkey and shenanigans, saying "I told you so! Jasper!" So, they would like to us to join the league of Socialist Nations and the sooner the better. I fear we are well onto that cobbled road.

But, meanwhile, for me, this is tripe since I wish us to retain all our power but to use it judiciously and where most needed. The meltdown of 2008 engendered by greed, that old artifice and strangler, not only should never have happened but it has hurt or clipped our standing in the world, the pecking order or how we rank among all the nations. We have got ourselves into this jam-up. I ask again: Was this mess a slip-up or something planned? I knew that we were off-guard; of course, we were unaware, and dumb as horses or cows. Our leaders, if they wish to save us and not watch passively more and greater train wrecks, must do colossally more to protect this nation, her people, her wealth. Telling the bankers to go to hell, to pound sand, to cram it, would be a good start. So, get right on it, will you, tanglefoot? Will you please?

And that small word, "please," reminds me of the past whose echoes, though faint, still course, and pound like blood in my veins. It is always good to say, 'please' when asking for a favor like General Omar N. Bradley did whenever he issued an order. Got that, my little buck pirate?

Having made this little spin or giro, we complete the circle by returning once more to the kind visage of my pop, that old, unmean, cogent navigator who said that to me long, big timber years ago. I was seated on his lap, the two of us occupying that one, large, red leather chair (back when chairs were solid, made of natured, dense hardwoods like hemlock or spruce, Bruce, not like today when so much is glued together with soft pine or particle board), I looking straight at the black and yellow MacLeod of Lewis plaid shirt on his chest, which made him look to me strong, stronger, strongest, like some demi-savage, Walter, or Irisher Robinson Crusoe, or better, since I knew already how smart he was, like some powerful king who would always help the meek and little people first. And then I, gazing up a little, towards his walnut Gaelic eyes which, in their turn, did gaze back down to me, studying me they are, so carefully and serenely watching me to see that I am paying proper attention (he called it then, "PPA"), and not going at all leftist or asleep, since he believed that all men ought to be able to make some decent money and to keep most of it, he measuring me all the times and keenly, as all fathers should, with his unwavering keen brown eyes; and then, I remember, as one does over the great gulf of time which becomes an inch, his saying a little later and quietly to me, in a king's voice, one which need not be raised, "Don't forget which I told you, Mister Greenhorn. Don't forget, remember. Do you hear me now? Don't you see?"

* * *

Remember what John Steinbeck writes to Adlai Stevenson in his letter, "Dear Adlai":

Mainly, Adlai, I am troubled by the cynical immorality of my country. I do not think it can survive on this basis and unless some kind of catastrophe strikes us, we are lost. But by our very attitudes we are drawing catastrophe to ourselves. What we have beaten in nature, we cannot conquer in ourselves.

Someone has to reinspect our system and that soon. We can't expect to raise our children to be good and honorable men when the city, the state, the government, the corporations all offer higher rewards for chicanery and deceit than probity and truth. On all levels it is rigged, Adlai. Maybe nothing can be done about it, but I am stupid enough and naively hopeful enough to want to try. How about you?

Yours,

John[25]

* * *

When: Subito - Immediately.

You have been waiting to talk to me for a long time.

Who are your friends?

Whenever there is easy money around...

Failure is not an option. Eugene Kranz of NASA, Operations Manager who helped to save Apollo 13

The nobles do nothing but talk ("Braveheart")
Or, swans swam; lords, lord. A small pebble goes a long ways. Only a direct, sharp attack wins. May I ask any question? The guy who seems to be the friend is not the friend, but a predator.

We have attacked ourselves.

* * *

---

25   "The Stevenson Letter." New Republic. 5 January, 1953: 13-14, taken from John Steinbeck: America and Americans. Edited by Susan Shillinglaw and Jackson J. Benson. Viking, NY 2002, p109

At the core of this interminable argument is the need for a fundamental rebellion, that is, to say, "No. No longer...", for, if we don't...

"We are dying." William Styron <u>Sophie's</u> <u>Choice</u>.

* * *

An English major surveys a scene of battle, and says:

"It is serious, but not desperate."

An Irish major regards the same field, and relates:

"It is desperate, but not serious."

That is, one has to get to the blessed point where you so not care one whit if it all goes away. The Irish have that concept in their bones: They <u>know</u> the world will disappoint, but that it is not the last one.

* * *

General George Smith Patten, Jr. comes to mind: His discipline, his determination to surmount difficulties, his belief that training leads to victory:

> "You must do your damndest and win. Remember, that is what you live.
>   Oh you must! You have got to do some thing! Never stop until you have gained the top or a grave." (P. 86)

> "YOU ARE NOT BEATEN UNTIL YOU ADMIT IT. HENCE, DON'T." (P. 306)

Carlo D'Este. <u>Patton</u>: <u>A</u> <u>Genius</u> <u>for</u>
<u>War</u>. Harper Collins: New York, NY,
1995.

Or from his cadet notebooks,

"By perseverance and study and eternal desire any
man can be great." (1906-1909)

And here, I must crudely paraphrase him:

The measure of a man is not whether he fails since
all men do.

What is important is that, after falling down, a
man gets up and tries again.

And so, in the face of all of this adversity, how does anyone
engender strength? It cannot come from me since I am weak
and my thoughts are paltry. One must pray for direction
and accede to God's will. Isaiah, "All good things come
by grace." (Norman Maclean. <u>A</u> <u>River</u> <u>Runs</u> <u>Through</u> <u>It</u>.)
God watches over us. My cousin, Bonnie writes to me of
her son: "He never complains, nor will I." We must breed a
greater toughness or tenacity, that ability to fight with the
gloves off.

And, beyond that, knowing that this world is near dark
and corrupt, and only my temporary one, I will pray to
Santa Lucia, the patron saint of light so that I might see
more clearly. Next, I will pray to Santa Rita, the patron
of impossible dreams, and, then, and only in Italian dopo
tutti angeli, i miei amici, al Santo Giuda, the patron saint
of lost causes. I ask: Is our country a lost cause, una causa
perduta?

Too, I recall with memory's compression of time, my
father's work with Father Patrick Peyton's campaign: "The

Family that Prays Together, Stays Together." I wonder: Would he be encouraged to guide today?

Also now, with jobs as scarce as snow in June, we have plenty of time to go often to the beach, the ocean, the sea. She is rejuvenating since, as Christopher Columbus knows, "The sea will grant each man new hope."

I understand now, after all of this worry and graum, that I must depart from them, that God has a golden plan for us, one which does not cost any money. Good! It is free, and I must train my mind and soul to trust it, and, then, to trust it even more. Prego: I pray. This is my prayer. O, hear my song, thou God of all the nations. Myself I give Thee; let Thy will be done, please. I will no longer search my paltry brain, but Yours. I will say it again, my paltry brain, and then, say yet again that accurate word: Paltry. Thus, Lord, you have shown me the only way home, and for this much I do thank you. I hear you say to all: "Come to me. I will give to you rest."

Bibliography

Ashbrook, Tom. *On Point*. March 31, 2009. Conversation with Simon Johnson *"Are the Banks running America?"*

Atkinson, Rick. *An Army at Dawn: The War in North Africa 1942-1943; Volume One of the Liberated Trilogy*. New York: Henry Holt and Company, 2002. Print.

Bartlett, John. *Bartlett's Familiar Quotations*. Morly, Christopher, Ed. Boston: Little Brown & Company, 1943. Print.

Bevington, David, Ed. *The Complete Works of William Shakespeare*. New York: Bantam Books, 1988. Print.

Blumenson, Martin. *The Patton Papers*, 1885-1940. Boston: Houghton Mifflin, 1972. Print.

Brewer's Dictionary of Phrase & Fable. Revised Ed. Ivor H. Evans, Ed. London: Cassell & Co., 1988. Print

Cohen, William D. *House of Cards: A Tale of Hubris and Wretched Excess on Wall Street*. New York: Doubleday, 2009. Print.

Davidoff, Nichols. *The Cather Was a Spy: The Mysterious Life of Moe Berg*. New York: Pantheon Books, 1994. Print.

Davis, Leslie. *Rivers in the Desert: William Mulholland and the Inventing of Los Angeles*. New York: Harper Collins, 1993. Print.

D'Este, Cards. *Patton: A Genius For War*. New York: Harper Perennial, 1996. Print.

Dickens, Paul, Ed. *War Slang: American Fighting Words and Phrases from the Civil War in Iraq*. 2nd Ed. New York: Bristol Park Books, 2007.

Dictionary of American Slang. New York: Crowell Publishers, 1975. Print

Farago, Ladislas. *The Last Days of Patton*. New York: McGraw Hill, 2007

Feldman, Ron J. and Gary H. Stern. *Too Big to Fail*. Washington, DC: Brookings Press, 2004. Print.

Flexner, Stuart Berg, and Harold Wentworth, Eds. *Dictionary of American Slang*. New York: Thomas Y. Crowell Company, 1975. Print.

Johnson, Simon blog of April 21, 2009. Conversation with Henry Blodget

Leaming, Barbara. *Jack Kennedy: The Education of a Statesman*. W.W. Norton & Co. New York, 2006.

Lebo, Harlan. *The Godfather Legacy*. New York: Fireside, 1997. Print.

Lowenstein, Roger. *When Genius Failed: The Rise and Fall of Long-Term Capitol Management*. New York: Random House, 2000. Print.

Nuttall, A.D. *Shakespeare: The Thinker*. New Haven and London: Yale University Press, 2007. Print.

Roubini, Nuriel. *Huffington Post Quotes*. April 4, 2009.

Sherrin, Ned, Ed. *The Oxford Dictionary of Humorous Quotations*. Third Edition. New York: Oxford University Press, 2005. Print.

Simpson, James B., Ed. *Simpson's Contemporary Quotations Revised*. New York: Harper Collins, 1997. Print.

Strausbaugh, John. *Sissy Nation: How America Became a Culture of Wimps and Stoopits*. New York: Virgin Books, 2007. Print.

Steinbeck, John. *America and Americans*. Edited by Susan Shillinglaw and Jackson J. Benson. New York: Viking Adult, 2002.

Stern, Gary H. and Feldman. *Too Big To Fail: The Hazards of Bank Bailouts*. Brookings Institution Press. Washington, DC 2004

Tosches, Nick. *King of the Jews*. New York: Harper Collins, 2005. Print.

Vaughan, Hal. *FDR's 12 Apostles: The Spies who paved the way for the Invasion of North Africa*. Guildford, Connecticut: The Lyons Press, 2006. Print.

History. The History Channel Magazine, September/October Edition, 2009. Periodical.

Shooting script of The Godfather. Margaret Herrick Library, Academy of Motion Pictures Arts and Sciences, March 29, 1971. Movie.